God's Unfolding Story of Salvation

God's Unfolding Story of Salvation

The Christ-Centered Biblical Storyline

Heather A. Kendall

RESOURCE *Publications* • Eugene, Oregon

GOD'S UNFOLDING STORY OF SALVATION
The Christ-Centered Biblical Storyline

Copyright © 2012 Heather A. Kendall. All rights reserved. Except for brief quotations in critical publications or reviews, no part of this book may be reproduced in any manner without prior written permission from the publisher. Write: Permissions, Wipf and Stock Publishers, 199 W. 8th Ave., Suite 3, Eugene, OR 97401.

Resource Publications
An imprint of Wipf and Stock Publishers
199 W. 8th Ave., Suite 3
Eugene, OR 97401

www.wipfandstock.com

isbn 13: 978-1-62032-046-4

Manufactured in the U.S.A.

Scripture quotations taken from The Holy Bible, New International Version® NIV®
Copyright© 1973, 1978, 1984, 2011 by Biblica, Inc.™
Used by permission. All rights reserved worldwide.

Thank you to my husband for his encouragement, and to the ladies' Tuesday morning Bible study for their helpful input.

Contents

List of Figures / ix
Introduction / xi

Part One — Preparing for the Promised Seed

Lesson 1 — The Beginning of the War: The Promised Seed / 17
Lesson 2 — Enoch and Noah: God's Gift of Faith / 21
Lesson 3 — Abraham: Preferring Spiritual Realities / 26
Lesson 4 — Melchizedek: Jesus, Our High Priest / 31
Lesson 5 — Isaac and Jacob: God's Grace in Conversion / 35
Lesson 6 — The Nation of Israel: Jesus, Our Passover Lamb / 39
Lesson 7 — The Sacrificial System: Spiritual Lessons in the Desert / 44
Lesson 8 — Ruth: Jesus, Our Kinsman-Redeemer / 48
Lesson 9 — King David: Assurance of Salvation / 52
Lesson 10 — David's Psalms: Communion with God / 56

Part Two — The Prophets: Waiting for the Promised Seed

Lesson 11 — The Prophets Elijah and Jonah: Responding to God's Message / 63
Lesson 12 — The Prophet Joel: The Battle Belongs to God / 67
Lesson 13 — The Prophets Amos and Hosea: Loving the Unlovely / 72
Lesson 14 — The Prophet Micah: Waiting for the Messiah / 78
Lesson 15 — The Prophet Isaiah: Our Greatest Need, Spiritual Salvation / 82
Lesson 16 — The Prophet Isaiah: Jesus, Mighty to Save / 87
Lesson 17 — The Prophets Zephaniah and Habakkuk: Persevering Faith / 91

Contents

    Lesson 18   The Prophet Jeremiah: A Circumcised Heart / 96

    Lesson 19   The Prophet Ezekiel: The Holy Spirit, Living Water / 101

    Lesson 20   The Prophet Daniel: Living by Faith, Not by Sight / 106

    Lesson 21   The Prophets Haggai and Zechariah: Obeying God / 110

    Lesson 22   The Prophets Malachi and John the Baptist: Witnessing for God / 114

Part Three   Jesus, the Promised Seed

    Lesson 23   The Birth of the Promised Seed: Responding to Jesus / 121

    Lesson 24   Jesus' Ministry: The Necessity of Spiritual Birth / 125

    Lesson 25   The Disciples of Jesus: Learning from the Master / 128

    Lesson 26   Mistaken Ideas about Jesus: Discerning the Truth / 133

    Lesson 27   Jesus: Nearing the End—Submitting to the Father's Will / 137

    Lesson 28   The Last Week of Jesus' Ministry: A Faithful Servant / 141

    Lesson 29   The Death of Jesus: Completing God's Plan / 146

    Lesson 30   The Resurrection and Ascension: A Time for Rejoicing / 151

Part Four   The Church: Proclaiming the Promised Seed

    Lesson 31   The Day of Pentecost: The Work of the Holy Spirit / 157

    Lesson 32   The Early Church: No Discrimination Allowed / 162

    Lesson 33   Growth through Missions: Resolving Conflict / 166

    Lesson 34   The Hope of Israel: A Believer's Hope / 169

    Lesson 35   Early Letters from Paul: Only One Gospel / 173

    Lesson 36   Later Letters from Paul: Salvation through Jesus Alone / 177

    Lesson 37   Letters from Other Authors: A Living Faith and Hope / 181

    Lesson 38   Revelation: Jesus, the Sovereign Lord / 186

Timeline / 191

Bibliography / 195

List of Figures

Compiled by Debra Kendall

1 World of the Founding Fathers / 26
2 World of Moses / 39
3 Empire of David and Solomon / 52
4 World of Jesus, the Promised Seed / 120

Introduction

Why Study Redemptive History

"You are worthy, our Lord and God, to receive glory and honor and power, for you created all things, and by your will they were created and have their being"

(REV 4:11).

ONE SUNNY AFTERNOON IN autumn my family and I parked our car and headed onto the Bruce Trail in southern Ontario. We entered the woods at the trailhead with only a few instructions obtained from the Internet—nothing else. My husband, daughter, and I were experienced hikers who should have known better. In the Rocky Mountains we always carried backpacks with emergency supplies. Yet on this day, we acted as if we were out for a short stroll in a city park. Once in the forest we wandered around in circles until my husband noticed the location of the sun. Using the sun as a bearing, he guided us onto the right path.

My family and I knew we were lost in the forest when we started to recognize certain trees for the second time. A well-worn expression came to mind: "You can't see the forest for the trees." While wandering among the trees, we could not tell the size or shape of the forest. Only an aerial view would be the best way to gain that sort of information.

The Bible is like a forest and individual books are similar to trees. Studying small portions of Scripture is worthwhile and necessary. Nevertheless one of the first steps of discipleship after salvation should be an understanding of the big picture in the Bible. This book will teach believers that the biblical storyline is Christ-centered.

As you progress through this study guide, you may feel as if you are in an airplane touching down randomly here and there. This is not the

Introduction

case. I pay close attention to the chronological order of events. As time passes, God builds on previous truths and explains more of his plan of salvation. Thus the New Testament interpretation of the Old Testament takes precedence.

Often people think of redemptive history only in terms of its promises in the Old Testament and its fulfillment in the New Testament. There is much more to the story than this. Throughout the Old Testament God the Father prepared for the coming of his Son, the promised seed. Furthermore in the Old Testament the Holy Spirit also pointed to Christ through direct prophecy, pictures or types, and anticipation.

As John Piper explains, "The term *redemptive history* simply refers to the history of God's acts recorded in the Bible. It is called redemptive history not because it isn't real history, but because it is history viewed from the perspective of God's redeeming purpose."[1] Written over a 1500-year period, the Bible explains how God has worked and is continuing to work throughout history to accomplish his plan of salvation.

The Lord wants us to know the whole tale. Otherwise he would not have given it to us. Moreover, since God's story ultimately affects each one of us, it is worth the time and effort required to understand it. If you do this, you will discover a pearl of great value. As you study, you will learn the steps God took to procure the spiritual salvation of believers—the most marvelous love story ever told. Forgiveness of sin and reconciliation with God are the greatest needs of everyone past, present, and future. This redemption story brings glory to God and benefits believers.

The Benefits of Understanding Redemptive History

After studying the big picture in the Bible, you will know God always tells the truth and always keeps his promises. He is reliable. The Lord loves and cares for everyone, but especially his own. Repetition aids in learning. Time after time God carries out his plan of salvation by working through ordinary people. Nothing or no one can thwart the sovereign God. He carried out his plan of salvation in spite of the opposition of Satan, his demons, and nonbelievers. Knowing these facts will reinforce your faith. It is also comforting. Whenever you are suffering in a difficult situation, you can count on God to lead you through the hard times.

---

1. Piper, *Desiring God*, 40n.

Introduction

The second benefit for understanding redemptive history is to keep from error. So many people, who have grown up in the church and have attended Sunday school regularly, have no idea of the timeline of the Bible. They may be very familiar with the major Bible stories, but they are unable to put those stories into historical context. Without a proper understanding of the biblical timeline, people may unwittingly develop tunnel vision. The result is a misunderstanding of Scripture when meditating on a particular passage. Therefore it is wise to keep the big picture in mind at all times. That is why I continually cross-reference related passages.

The third benefit for understanding redemptive history is to gain an overwhelming desire for evangelism because we love others and want them to repent of their sin and trust our Savior. This is what characterized the early church, and it should be the same for us. Those early believers loved the lost, prayed, and witnessed to their unsaved friends and neighbors.

The most important reason for understanding redemptive history is to gain an appreciation of Jesus' sovereignty. While Jesus was alive, he promised his disciples that he would build his church and the gates of hell would not prevail against it. After his death and resurrection, God exalted Jesus and gave him all authority. As creator, he is king over all. However, by his death and resurrection, Jesus became the king promised in the Old Testament. Because of his authority we can be assured that the church will continue to grow until the end of time.

Guidelines for Group Study

"But when he, the Spirit of truth, comes, he will guide you into all truth"

(JOHN 16:13).

I designed this study for small groups of believers, both older teenagers, and adults. That is why there is an icebreaking question at the beginning of each lesson. To be effective, everyone must be willing to invest time in individual Bible reading and in answering the questions at home. Some lessons do require a lot of reading and flipping to several books in the Bible. Everyone should also make a commitment to work on every lesson in the proper order. This is very necessary because each lesson builds on

Introduction

the previous one. Not completing a lesson would be like building a house and ignoring one of the support beams.

I have divided the lessons into four parts: "Preparing for the Promised Seed"; "The Prophets: Waiting for the Promised Seed"; "Jesus, the Promised Seed"; and "The Church: Proclaiming the Promised Seed." You will receive the most benefit by completing this study as one unit. If the group wants to take a break, however, you may stop at the end of one of those parts.

You will find a title and subtitle for each lesson. The title points to the timeline of the Bible. The subtitle describes the spiritual application of that particular lesson. Because each lesson does have a spiritual application, guests who come to the group will benefit.

Leaders and teachers, make sure no one dominates the group discussion. You need to know if everyone understands what the Bible teaches at that point in history. If you have nonbelievers in your group, pray that the Holy Spirit will speak to them, convict them of their sin, and their need for the Savior.

PART ONE

Preparing for the Promised Seed

Lesson 1

The Beginning of the War: The Promised Seed

BEFORE THE BIRTH OF my first child, I panicked when someone told me that my philodendron had poisonous leaves. Therefore I packed up all my plants and stored them at my mother-in-law's house in a distant city. I did not want my child to eat the poisonous leaves and die. I also wanted to avoid fighting with my toddler.

Question: How do you react to confrontation?

Paradise

READ PS 148:1–13

1. List everything God created.

READ GEN 1:31—2:1

2. What kind of world did God create?

Paradise Lost

READ GEN 3:1–5; REV 12:7–9

1. Who is the serpent in the Garden of Eden?

2. What did the serpent ask Eve?

3. How did she respond?

4. How did the serpent undermine God's authority?

READ GEN 3:6–13

5. What happened as soon as they ate the forbidden fruit?

READ GEN 3:14, 15

6. What did God promise Adam and Eve, which gave them hope for reconciliation?

READ GEN 3:16–24

7. What were the consequences of their disobedience?

8. Why did God shed the blood of an animal?

READ LUKE 4:5–7; JOHN 8:44; JOHN 12:31; 1 JOHN 5:19

9. How did the sin of Adam and Eve benefit Satan?

Cain and Abel

READ GEN 4:1–7; 1 SAM 16:7

1. What sacrifices did Cain and Abel bring to God?

2. Why did Abel's sacrifice please God, but Cain's did not?

READ GEN 4:8, 9

3. How did Cain react to God's plea not to be angry?

4. Both brothers shed blood. What was the difference?

READ GEN 4:10–12

5. What was Cain's punishment?

READ HEB 11:1, 2, 4; JUDE 10, 11; 1 JOHN 3:12

6. Why did God declare Abel righteous?

7. What kingdom did each of the brothers belong to?

Application: The Old Testament points to Jesus through preparation for his birth, direct prophecy, pictures or types, and anticipation. Which of these apply in this lesson?

Reflection: How do you know if you need a Savior?

Summary

After God created the heavens and the earth, God saw everything he had made. It was very good, including Satan. When Satan initiated a rebellion in heaven, he did not surprise God. No one, not even Satan, can thwart God's plans.

Later on Satan succeeded in tricking Adam and Eve into rebelling against the Lord. The consequence was physical and spiritual death for the human race. Once again God knew beforehand what would happen. Not caught unawares, he immediately set his plan of salvation into motion. First the Lord promised to send the Savior. Then he shed the blood of an animal for its hide to cover their naked bodies. Ever since Adam and Eve's rebellion, God has required the shedding of blood to atone for sin.

Because of Satan's rebellion, God and Satan formed their battle lines. Cain and Abel are evidence of this. As a result some have longed for the Savior to restore them to fellowship with God while others have not. The only hope of humanity lay in the coming of the promised seed. That is why no one can avoid confrontation in this world.

Lesson 2

Enoch and Noah: God's Gift of Faith

How often have you heard someone lament that the world appears more evil than years ago? Have you ever wondered why? We live in a fallen state in which the world, the flesh, and the devil constantly strive to make the earth a worse place than previously.

Question: What is an example of sin's downward spiral?

Enoch

According to Genesis 5, there are 622 years between the creation of Adam and Enoch's birth.

READ GEN 5:1–31; HEB 11:5, 6

1. What happened to every man except Enoch?

2. What happened to Enoch?

3. Why did God treat Enoch differently from the others?

God's Unfolding Story of Salvation

4. What are the prerequisites of faith in God?

Noah

According to Genesis 5, there are 1034 years between Enoch's birth and the flood. Noah was 600 years old at the time of the flood (Gen 7:6).

READ GEN 6:5–13

1. How did God feel about his creation? Why?

2. What did God decide to do about it?

3. Why did God spare Noah?

READ GEN 6:3

4. How much time did God give the people to admit their wickedness and repent (turn from their sin and obey God)?

READ GEN 6:14–17, 21, 22

5. How did Noah prepare for the flood?

Enoch and Noah: God's Gift of Faith

READ GEN 7:1–12; 2 PET 2:5

6. Who entered the ark?

7. Explain why nobody else did.

8. Name the two groups of people.

READ GEN 7:17–24

9. How did God punish those people?

READ GEN 8:18–22

10. What was God's covenant with Noah?

11. Who determined the terms of this covenant?

12. What blood did Noah shed to ratify, or guarantee, the fulfillment of this covenant?

God's Unfolding Story of Salvation

READ GEN 9:8–17

13. What is the sign of this covenant?

14. Explain how God has kept his promise so far with respect to this covenant.

READ HEB 11:7

15. Why did Noah build the ark?

16. How did God reward him?

Application: The Old Testament points to Jesus through preparation for his birth, direct prophecy, pictures or types, and anticipation. Which of these apply in this lesson?

Reflection: Faith involves obeying God and ignoring peer pressure. Do others easily influence your opinions?

Summary

For over 1600 years most people rebelled against God in their thought life and in their actions. Very few exhibited any faith in God. Enoch and Noah were different, thus proving faith truly is a gift of God. Before people will care about their need for a Savior, the Holy Spirit must lovingly open their spiritual eyes.

Enoch and Noah: God's Gift of Faith

By Noah's day the world had become so evil that God's judgment overrode mercy. The Lord will not and cannot ignore rebellion forever. When he spared Noah and his family, God taught us an important lesson. One day God will judge the wicked and find them guilty of sin. But he will protect those who trust in him.

Lesson 3

Abraham: Preferring Spiritual Realities

Abraham: 1951–1776 BC (Gen 25:7).[1]

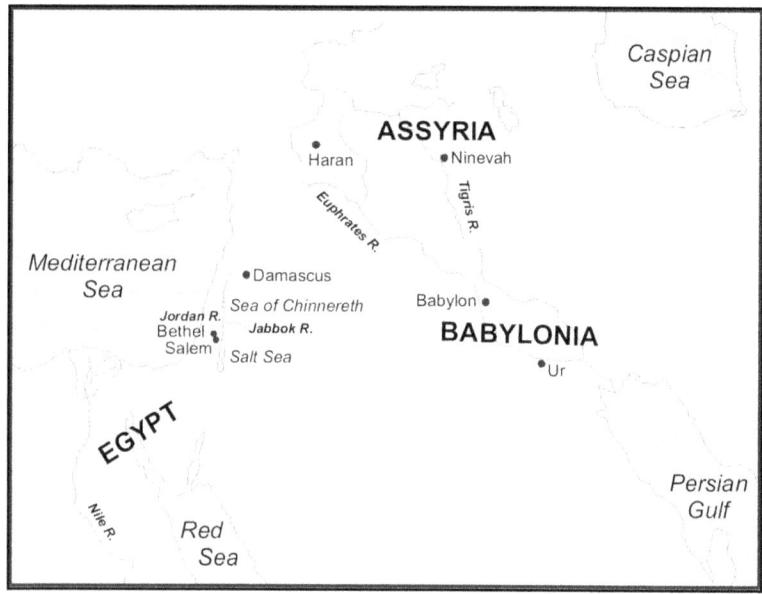

Figure 1: World of the Founding Fathers[2]

IMAGINE YOURSELF IN THE country or backwoods and far from city lights. Then turn on your flashlight or light a kerosene lamp. No matter how dim the light, it still illuminates the darkness. The founding fathers of the faith were lights in a dark world.

---

1. Kendall, *A Tale of Two Kingdoms*, 41.
2. Ibid., 41.

Question: How can you tell the difference between one who believes in God and one who does not?

Abram, 1876 BC[3]

READ GEN 11:31—12:5; GAL 3:8, 9

1. What physical blessings did God promise Abram?

2. What spiritual blessings did God promise him?

READ JOSH 24:2, 3

3. Why was Abram's move to Canaan so significant?

READ HEB 11:8–10, 13–16

4. What was Abram thinking while he was a stranger in a foreign land?

God's Covenant with Abram

READ GEN 15:1–6

1. What was Abram's problem?

2. How did he propose to solve this problem?

---

3. Ibid., 416.

God's Unfolding Story of Salvation

3. Why did God declare Abram righteous?

READ GEN 15:7–12, 17, 18

4. What was God's covenant with Abram?

5. What blood did Abram shed to ratify, or guarantee, the fulfillment of this covenant?

READ 1 CHR 13:5; 2 SAM 8:3–6; NEH 9:7, 8

6. Compare the land promised with the land received.

The Everlasting Covenant, 1852 BC[4]

READ GEN 17:1–7

1. Why did God change Abram's name to Abraham?

READ GEN 22:15–18; ACTS 3:24–26

2. Who is the seed who would carry out God's plan of salvation?

---

4. Ibid., 46.

Abraham: Preferring Spiritual Realities

READ GAL 3:13–18

3. Whose blood was shed to ratify, or guarantee, the spiritual aspect of this covenant?

4. What did Jesus' death accomplish for believers?

READ ROM 4:16–18; GAL 3:6, 7

5. Who are Abraham's spiritual children?

READ GEN 17:8–14

6. What did God promise Abraham's physical descendants?

7. Why did God require the circumcision of all males?

8. What would happen to those who were not circumcised?

READ GEN 2:16, 17

9. Compare the commandment given in the Garden of Eden to circumcision.

God's Unfolding Story of Salvation

Application: The Old Testament points to Jesus through preparation for his birth, direct prophecy, pictures or types, and anticipation. Which of these apply in this lesson?

Reflection: What do your actions reveal about your priorities?

Summary

When Abraham moved from Ur in Babylonia and later from Haran in Assyria, he left people who worshiped the moon.[5] He followed God's leading without knowing where he would end up. In Hebrews, the Lord commended Abraham's faith and pointed out how Abraham cared more about spiritual realities than earthly concerns. Moreover Abraham's spiritual children will always be like-minded. This sin-filled world is only our temporary dwelling place. We look forward to a sin-free world where God will dwell with us forever. This kind of faith results in an overwhelming desire to please God at any cost.

God did promise to bless Abraham's physical descendants with the land of Canaan, forever. Through the battles won by David, God's people eventually conquered all the Promised Land. Yet, in order to retain these physical promises, God required the circumcision of every boy baby. Furthermore, when God founded the nation of Israel 400 years later, he declared they must keep all of his laws, not just the act of physical circumcision. Disobedience meant loss of blessing. In contrast, God's people would never lose the spiritual benefits of this covenant because Jesus' blood guaranteed their fulfillment.

Jews today still regard God's promise of land as relevant to them. They think since God promised them the land forever, they deserve it, no matter how they behave. They refuse to accept the fact that God's promise of land is conditional. Disobedience still means loss of blessing. Worse, they are blind to the new reality—blessing only comes by trusting in the finished work of Christ on Calvary and by obeying him.

---

5. Robinson, "History of the Hebrew and Jewish People," 61.

Lesson 4

Melchizedek: Jesus, Our High Priest

MELCHIZEDEK WAS THE KING-PRIEST of Salem over 400 years before Israel would become a nation and over 800 years before David would make Jerusalem his capital.

Sometimes labor disputes drag on for months. If both sides do not compromise and come to an agreement, they may ask an arbitrator to intervene and negotiate a settlement. The arbitrator functions as a mediator between both parties.

Question: When have you settled disagreements between two people?

READ GEN 14:1–16

1. What happened to Abram's nephew Lot?

2. How did Abram rescue Lot and the others?

READ GEN 14:17–20

3. How did Melchizedek celebrate the victory with Abram?

God's Unfolding Story of Salvation

4. Why did Melchizedek bless Abram?

5. Who was responsible for Abram's victory in battle?

6. How did Abram respond to Melchizedek's blessing?

READ HEB 7:1–3

7. What does Melchizedek's name mean?

8. What does Salem mean?

9. Compare Melchizedek and Jesus.

READ HEB 7:4

10. Why was Melchizedek so important?

READ HEB 7:5–10

11. What did the Levitical priests receive from the Israelites?

12. Why could Melchizedek bless Abram?

Melchizedek: Jesus, Our High Priest

13. What was the difference between Melchizedek and Levi?

14. Explain why Melchizedek's actions demonstrated superiority over the Levitical priests.

READ HEB 7:11–17

15. Why were the Levites priests?

16. Why were Melchizedek and Jesus priests?

READ HEB 7:18–28

17. Why is Jesus a superior high priest?

READ 1 TIM 2:5; ROM 1:1–4

18. Who is the only mediator between God and people?

19. Explain why Jesus is qualified to be the only mediator for sinners.

READ PS 110:4; HEB 5:5, 6

20. Who decreed Jesus would be a high priest forever?

Application: The Old Testament points to Jesus through preparation for his birth, direct prophecy, pictures or types, and anticipation. Which of these apply in this lesson?

Reflection: Whom do you rely on to be your mediator with God? Why?

Summary

God blessed Abram through Melchizedek. In return Abram acknowledged God had given him the victory over his enemies. He worshiped the Lord by giving one tenth of his spoils to Melchizedek. Later Scripture explains the significance of this incident.

Since Melchizedek represents the everlasting priesthood of Jesus, this story reveals an important step in redemptive history. Sin has separated us from God. Therefore we need a representative to offer a sacrifice acceptable to God. Jesus is the only high priest qualified to be an eternal arbitrator between sinners and God. We need no other ever.

Lesson 5

Isaac and Jacob: God's Grace in Conversion

Most parents want their children to follow their religious beliefs. Some diligently teach their children while others think they will learn by example. Other parents deliberately teach nothing spiritual so that their children will have the freedom to believe whatever they want.

Question: Which method of childrearing do you prefer?

Isaac, 1851–1671 BC[1]

READ GEN 18:10–12; GEN 21:1–5

1. How was God gracious to Sarah?

2. What happened to Isaac when he was eight days old? Why?

READ GEN 22:1–19

3. How did God test the faith of Abraham and Isaac?

---

1. Kendall, *A Tale of Two Kingdoms*, 419.

God's Unfolding Story of Salvation

4. What did God promise Abraham because he had obeyed?

READ HEB 11:17–19; JOHN 3:16

5. What was Abraham thinking as he raised the knife in the air?

6. Compare this story with Jesus' death on the cross.

Jacob, 1791–1644 BC[2]

READ GEN 25:21–28

1. Which twin did God ordain would be stronger? This boy would be next in the line of promise.

READ GEN 27:1–40

2. What did Jacob do in order to receive Isaac's blessing?

3. How did Isaac and Esau react when they found out what had happened?

READ GEN 27:41–28:5

4. What happened because of Jacob's deception?

---

2. Ibid., 419.

Isaac and Jacob: God's Grace in Conversion

READ GEN 32:3–21

5. Jacob was about to meet Esau again after twenty years of separation. How did he feel? What did he do?

READ GEN 32:22–33:11

6. What was Jacob's new name? Why?

7. How did Jacob show through his actions that he was a changed man after his wrestling match?

READ GEN 49:10

8. What did Jacob prophesy for his son Judah?

READ 1 SAM 17:12[3]; MATT 1:1; MATT 28:18, 19; PHIL 2:9–11

9. How did Jesus fulfill these promises?

---

3. Ephrath is another name for Bethlehem (Gen 35:19).

Application: The Old Testament points to Jesus through preparation for his birth, direct prophecy, pictures or types, and anticipation. Which of these apply in this lesson?

Reflection: Jacob is proof that no one is too wicked to be saved. How did your behavior change after you trusted Jesus as your Savior?

Summary

The Lord chose Abraham, Isaac, and Jacob as the patriarchs or founding fathers of the faith. Through them God began to prepare for the coming of the promised seed, the Savior. By asking Abraham to sacrifice his only son on Mount Moriah, the Lord provided the first clue about his plan of salvation. Just as Abraham was willing to sacrifice his only son, God the Father would do likewise. Furthermore, when Jesus died on the cross, he took the place of sinners. In the same way the ram replaced Isaac on the altar. Of course, Abraham did not understand the implications of this traumatic event in his life. He only believed God would not allow the child of promise to die.

Moreover God illustrated his grace and mercy in conversion when he saved Jacob. Before Jacob wrestled with God, he was a liar and a cheat, consumed with self-interest. Afterward Jacob cared more about his family's safety than his own. Although Jacob still feared Esau's wrath, he told Esau the truth.

On Jacob's deathbed, God revealed the next link in his plan of salvation would be Jacob's son, Judah. A king would be born who would rule over all nations. That is why the Israelites were so careful to keep accurate genealogic records.

Lesson 6

The Nation of Israel: Jesus, Our Passover Lamb

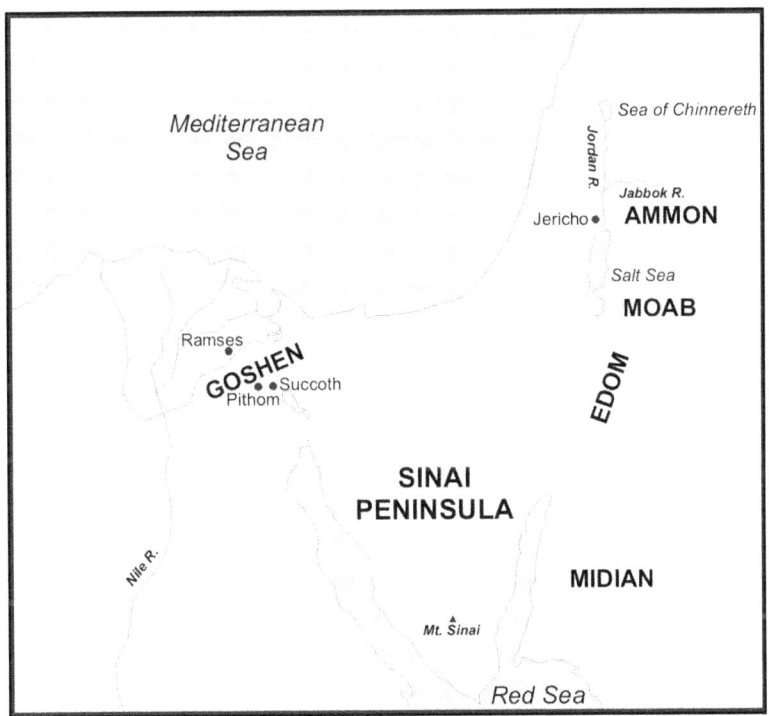

Figure 2: World of Moses[1]

NOBODY LIKES RULES OR ultimatums. Even worse, we dislike whenever someone catches and punishes us. Recall the child caught with a hand in the cookie jar. Looking up sheepishly, the child asks, "What's wrong, Mom?"

---

1. Kendall, *A Tale of Two Kingdoms*, 61.

God's Unfolding Story of Salvation

Question: Describe difficulties you have faced in correcting bad behavior.

Escape from Egypt, 1446 BC[2]

READ EXOD 11:1, 4–7

1. What was the last plague God brought on the Egyptians?

READ EXOD 12:1–13

2. How were the Israelites to prepare and celebrate the Passover?

3. What was the importance of the blood on the doorframes?

READ EXOD 12:31–33

4. How did Pharaoh and the Egyptians react to this plague?

READ EXOD 14:19–31

5. How did the Israelites cross the Red Sea safely?

6. What happened to Pharaoh and his army when they tried to cross?

---

2. Ibid., 417.

The Nation of Israel: Jesus, Our Passover Lamb

READ JOHN 1:29; 1 COR 5:7; 1 PET 1:18–21

7. Why is Jesus the superior Passover Lamb?

8. When did God make his plans to correct the problem of sin?

9. What is God's plan of salvation?

The Covenant at Sinai, 1446 BC[3]

READ EXOD 19:1–8

1. What did God promise the Israelites?

2. What condition did God attach to this covenant?

3. How did the people respond to this condition?

READ EXOD 19:16–19

4. What happened when God descended to the top of Mount Sinai?

---

3. Ibid., 417.

God's Unfolding Story of Salvation

READ EXOD 20:1–21

5. How did the Israelites react when God spoke the Ten Commandments to them?

6. How did Moses respond?

READ EXOD 24:3–8

7. What blood did the Israelites shed to ratify, or guarantee, the fulfillment of this covenant?

8. What did the Israelites promise God?

READ EXOD 24:12–18

9. What did God give Moses? Why?

10. How long did Moses stay on the mountain?

READ EXOD 32:1–8

11. What did the Israelites do while Moses was gone? Why?

Application: The Old Testament points to Jesus through preparation for his birth, direct prophecy, pictures or types, and anticipation. Which of these apply in this lesson?

Reflection: Are we any different from the Israelites? How patient are we when God makes us wait? Do we disappoint God and disobey even though we sincerely intend to obey?

Summary

In the Passover lamb, we catch the next glimpse of God's intent for his plan of salvation. The blood of the Passover lamb protected the firstborn boy from physical death as long as he stayed inside the house. In contrast, the blood of Jesus covers believers and protects them from spiritual death.

After the Exodus from Egypt, God established Israel as his special people, a nation separated from the rest of the world. He formally declared his covenant with them at Mount Sinai. There on that mountaintop God wrote the Ten Commandments, or the terms of this covenant, on two stone tablets. The Lord had two reasons for setting the Israelites apart as his own. First, God needed the promised seed to belong to a nation and a family. Secondly, for the first time in history, God revealed his laws so that people would begin to understand what sin entailed.

The Israelites joyfully told God that they would obey. Although sincere, they failed miserably. At the first opportunity they ignored God's warnings and committed idolatry. Thus they demonstrated how impossible it is for us to work for our salvation. Any attempt fails and falls short of God's glory.

LESSON 7

The Sacrificial System: Spiritual Lessons in the Desert

ONE OF JOB'S SO-CALLED friends, Eliphaz, lamented, "Yet man is born to trouble as surely as sparks fly upward" (Job 5:7). Everyone experiences trouble in this life. No one is immune. Some face sickness or financial woes; others suffer famine, attacks by wild animals, persecution or war.

Question: Why is it easier to learn spiritual lessons in bad times than in good?

The Day of Atonement

READ LEV 16:1–19

1. What did the high priest do inside the Most Holy Place?

2. What did the sacrificed goat represent?

READ LEV 16:20–33

3. What happened to the live goat?

The Sacrificial System: Spiritual Lessons in the Desert

4. What did the scapegoat signify?

READ LEV 16:34; HEB 9:7–10

5. How often did God allow the high priest to go into the Holy of Holies?

6. What does the word "atonement" mean?

7. What was the purpose of the Day of Atonement?

READ HEB 9:23–28

8. Why is Jesus' sacrifice superior?

9. Compare the high priest with Jesus.

10. Compare the two goats with Jesus.

READ HEB 10:1–4

11. What was the purpose of the sacrificial system?

God's Unfolding Story of Salvation

READ ROM 5:8–11

12. What did Jesus' death and resurrection accomplish for believers?

The Bronze Snake, 1407 BC[1]

READ NUM 21:4–9

1. Why were the Israelites complaining?

2. To whom were they complaining?

3. What did God do to punish them?

4. What did Moses pray?

5. What was God's response to Moses' prayer?

READ JOHN 3:14, 15

6. How is Jesus like the bronze snake?

---

1. Kendall, *A Tale of Two Kingdoms*, 77.

Application: The Old Testament points to Jesus through preparation for his birth, direct prophecy, pictures or types, and anticipation. Which of these apply in this lesson?

Reflection: False religions encourage people to work for their salvation. Why is it so difficult to admit spiritual helplessness?

Summary

At Mount Sinai, God had instructed Moses on how to set up an elaborate sacrificial system. In so doing, the Lord reminded the Israelites constantly of their need for a sacrificial substitute to pay the penalty for their sin. Moreover once a year, on the Day of Atonement, the high priest entered the Most Holy Place to atone for his sins and those of the people. The two goats represented two aspects of Jesus' substitutionary sacrifice. The first goat shed his blood for the people while the scapegoat carried their guilt far away. Jesus accomplished salvation for his people once for all time whereas the high priest had to repeat the ceremony annually.

For thirty-nine years God had provided clear expectations for the Israelites' behavior through the law. He also declared his love for them and gracious forgiveness of their sins by the sacrificial system. Since the Israelites continued to complain throughout their desert wanderings, the Lord sent poisonous snakes into the camp. Before they entered the Promised Land, God reminded them of their helplessness and inability to save themselves. Likewise, we are dependent on the finished work of Jesus on Calvary for our spiritual salvation.

Lesson 8

Ruth: Jesus, Our Kinsman-Redeemer

Ruth lived during the time of the Judges (Ruth 1:1; 1375–1050 BC).[1] Date written: Sometime after David became king.

THESE DAYS MOST PEOPLE in developed countries move for one of two reasons. Some relocate to start a new job or go to college or university. Others want to change the size of their house or move from an apartment to a house. Seniors often downsize whereas those with young families buy bigger houses.

Question: Why did you move last?

READ RUTH 1:1–7

1. Why did Elimelech and his family leave Judah?

READ RUTH 1:8–22

2. How did Ruth respond when Naomi told her to return to her own people?

3. What did Naomi tell her friends after she had returned to Bethlehem?

---

1. Maas, "A Chronology of Bible Events and World Events," 421.

Ruth: Jesus, Our Kinsman-Redeemer

READ LEV 19:9, 10

4. How were landowners to take care of those in need?

READ RUTH 2:1–16

5. Why did Boaz take such good care of Ruth?

READ RUTH 2:17–23

6. Why was Naomi glad that Boaz had treated Ruth so kindly?

READ RUTH 3:1–9

7. What instructions did Naomi give Ruth?

8. What reason did Ruth give Boaz for lying at his feet?

READ RUTH 3:10–18

9. How did Boaz react?

READ RUTH 4:1–12; NUM 27:1–11; DEUT 25:5, 6

10. What legal transaction took place at the town gate?

11. Explain the functions of a kinsman-redeemer.

God's Unfolding Story of Salvation

READ RUTH 4:13–22

12. How did God bless Naomi and Ruth?

13. What is Ruth's relationship to King David?

READ ACTS 20:28; COL 1:13, 14

14. What does the word "redemption" mean?

15. What did Jesus buy? How?

16. What blessings do believers possess because Jesus bought us?

Application: The Old Testament points to Jesus through preparation for his birth, direct prophecy, pictures or types, and anticipation. Which of these apply in this lesson?

Reflection: How willing are you to step out in faith like Ruth?

Summary

The kinsman-redeemer is a picture of what Jesus would do for his people in the spiritual realm. Jesus left the glory of heaven to come to earth to redeem a people for God. Jesus paid the required price with his blood whereas Boaz paid money for Ruth.

The kinsman-redeemer did not have to accept this role. The closest relative to Ruth and Naomi refused to accept it. Similarly, Jesus did not have to become our Redeemer. Like Boaz, he willingly and gladly accepted it. Because of Jesus' death and resurrection, believers enjoy all the rights and privileges of God's children. Our Redeemer has restored us to fellowship with God.

LESSON 9

King David: Assurance of Salvation

Reign of David: 1010–970 BC[1]

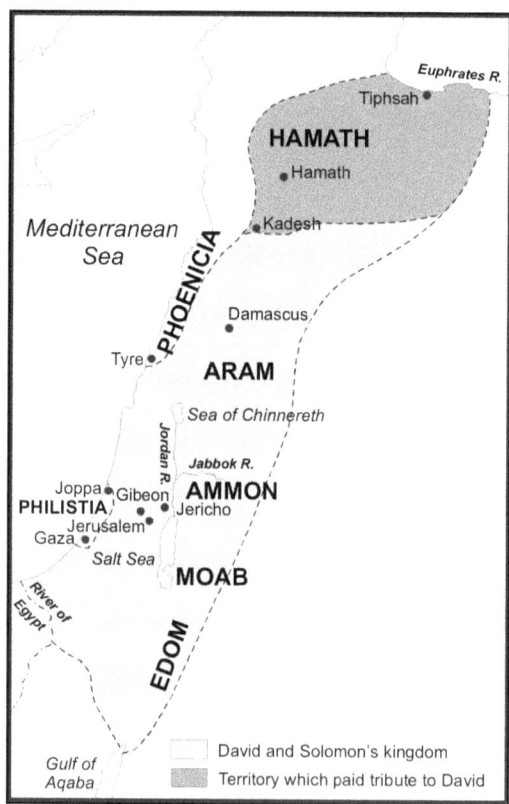

Figure 3: Empire of David and Solomon[2]

GOD GAVE MY CHURCH over nine acres of land and several used portables in which to worship him. After a few years, repairs for the buildings

---

1. Maas, "A Chronology of Bible Events and World Events," 431.
2. Kendall, *A Tale of Two Kingdoms*, 86.

became too costly because of their old age. We needed a permanent structure. Therefore the head of the building committee challenged everyone to sacrifice his or her best in order to raise money for God's house.

Question: What kind of sacrifices have you made for your family or for God?

A Man after God's Own Heart

READ 1 SAM 17:1–50

1. What did David care most about?

2. How much was he willing to risk for God?

The Worship of the Lord in Zion (Jerusalem)

READ 1 CHR 15:1–3

1. What did David do?

READ 1 CHR 16:1–4, 37–40

2. How did David worship God in Zion?

3. Explain how David obeyed God in Gibeon.

God's Unfolding Story of Salvation

READ PS 51:15–17

4. What sacrifices please God?

READ HEB 12:22–24

5. What is significant about the word "Zion"?

God's Covenant with David

READ 2 SAM 7:8–16; PS 132:11, 12

1. What did God promise David?

2. What condition did God require of David's descendants in order to remain on the throne?

READ LUKE 1:26–33; HEB 1:8

3. Who would receive David's throne and reign forever?

READ ISA 55:3; ACTS 13:34; HEB 13:20, 21

4. How did God fulfill his promise to David?

5. Whose blood was shed to ratify, or guarantee, the fulfillment of the everlasting covenant?

The Last Words of David

READ 2 SAM 23:1–7; PS 25:1–11

1. What assurance of spiritual salvation did David have? Why?

2. What happens to those who do not believe in God?

Application: The Old Testament points to Jesus through preparation for his birth, direct prophecy, pictures or types, and anticipation. Which of these apply in this lesson?

Reflection: How can you have assurance of salvation?

Summary

Over 630 years earlier, God had promised Jacob that a line of kings would arise from his son Judah. When David became king, God began to keep this promise. Later on, God made a covenant with David that a coming king would reign forever. This covenant was the next step in God's plan of salvation.

    A man after God's own heart, David yearned to worship God in spirit and in truth. That is why he pitched a tent at Jerusalem, or Zion, where he could exalt God. For this reason the word "Zion" came to mean the place of spiritual worship from that time on in the Scriptures. In spite of this, David never neglected worshiping the Lord in Gibeon, according to the sacrificial requirements of the Old Covenant.

    On his deathbed David had complete confidence that God would provide for his salvation. He understood God's covenant with him was everlasting, arranged, and secure in every part. These are the sure mercies of David. It is our sure mercy, also.

LESSON 10

David's Psalms: Communion with God

WRITING REVEALS THE HEART of the author. Your loved ones may treasure your journal or diary after you are gone. Yet some people may hesitate to write down what they are feeling. King David wrote many psalms—some concerning the Savior.

Question: Do you learn best by writing or in some other way?

Psalm 22

1. Describe the sufferings of Jesus prophesied by David.

Psalm 22	New Testament	Fulfillment
Ps 22:1	Matt 27:46	
Ps 22:7, 8	Matt 27:41–43	
Ps 22:15	John 19:28	
Ps 22:16	John 20:24–28	
Ps 22:17	John 19:31–33 Luke 23:35	
Ps 22:18	Matt 27:35	

READ PS 22:30, 31; MATT 5:17; LUKE 24:44–47; JOHN 19:30

2. What did Jesus finish?

Psalm 110

READ PS 110:1, 2; ACTS 2:33–36

1. Who are the two Lords in this psalm?

2. What did God the Father promise Jesus?

READ MATT 22:41–45; HEB 1:1–3

3. What did Jesus teach the Pharisees?

Psalm 16

READ PS 16:8–11; ACTS 2:22–32; MARK 16:19

1. What did God promise his Holy One?

2. Describe the fulfillment of this psalm.

3. When did Jesus receive the throne of David?

4. Where is Jesus' throne?

Psalm 2

READ PS 2:1–3; ACTS 4:23–29

1. Who were the first rulers to plot against Jesus?

READ REV 19:11–21

2. Who will be the last rulers to challenge him?

3. What will happen to them?

READ PS 2:4–7; ACTS 13:26–33

4. Why did God laugh at the rulers?

5. What good news did God promise the Israelites?

6. How do we know Jesus is God's Son?

READ PHIL 2:5–11

7. How did Jesus become king?

READ PS 2:8–12; REV 2:26–29; MATT 28:16–20

8. What authority does Jesus have now?

Application: The Old Testament points to Jesus through preparation for his birth, direct prophecy, pictures or types, and anticipation. Which of these apply in this lesson?

Reflection: Do you seek daily to commune with your Lord through prayer and Bible study? If not, why not?

Summary

David had such a close relationship with the Lord that God revealed more precious truths to him about Jesus, the promised seed. For example, God taught David that Jesus is fully God and fully man. Moreover God laughs at rulers who think they can foil his plans. Those rulers may think they are in charge of their own destiny. But God is sovereign. After his death and resurrection, God the Son would receive his kingdom and then sit on David's throne forever.

The Holy Spirit taught David all those truths 1000 years before Jesus' birth. Of course, David did not understand exactly how the Savior would pay for his sin and reconcile him to God. He did believe it would happen.

PART TWO

The Prophets: Waiting for the Promised Seed

Lesson 11

The Prophets Elijah and Jonah: Responding to God's Message

MANY PEOPLE ARE WILLING to give others advice whether it is asked for or not. Some advice is wise; some is foolish. Governments have fallen, churches have split, and families have broken up after someone followed bad advice. Because of his son Solomon's sin, God allowed David's grandson Rehoboam to heed bad advice. The result was disastrous for God's people.

Question: Can you give examples of some bad advice that have caused problems in families?

The Division of Israel, 930 BC[1]

READ 1 KGS 12:1–17

1. What bad advice did Rehoboam's friends give him?

2. What happened when Rehoboam listened to them?

READ 1 KGS 12:25–33

---

1. Maas, "A Chronology of Bible Events and World Events," 431.

God's Unfolding Story of Salvation

3. What was Jeroboam afraid of?

4. How did he decide to solve his problem?[2]

5. How would you describe Jeroboam's influence on the Israelites?

Elijah on Mount Carmel

This event occurred during the reign of Ahab, king of Israel: 874–853 BC[3]

READ 1 KGS 16:29–33; 1 KGS 17:1; JAS 5:17, 18

1. Why did God send a famine on Israel?

2. How long did the famine last?

READ 1 KGS 18:16–18

3. Who did Ahab blame for the famine?

READ 1 KGS 18:19–40

4. How did Elijah challenge the prophets of Baal?

---

2. Bethel was a town in the southern part of Israel while Dan was located in the north.
3. Maas, "A Chronology of Bible Events and World Events," 598.

The Prophets Elijah and Jonah: Responding to God's Message

5. What happened when the prophets of Baal called on their god?

6. What happened when Elijah prayed to God?

7. How did God deal with those responsible for leading Israel into idolatry?

Jonah, the First Missionary

Date written: about 785–760 BC[4]
Reign of Jeroboam II: 793–753 BC[5]

READ JONAH 3:1—4:3

1. God sent Jonah to warn the Ninevites. What was Jonah's message?

2. How did the Ninevites react to his preaching?

3. Why was Jonah angry at God's response?

READ JER 18:7–10

4. What is God's law for nations?

---

4. Ibid., 1559.
5. Ibid., 1559.

5. Why did God's mercy overrule his justice for the Ninevites?

Application: The Old Testament points to Jesus through preparation for his birth, direct prophecy, pictures or types, and anticipation. Which of these apply in this lesson?

Reflection: How are you reacting to God's word?

Summary

The Israelites and Ninevites illustrated two possible responses to God's message. Sadly, those who rejected the truth had the greatest opportunity to receive it, for they were God's special people. Many years later, the Lord would warn Judah through the prophet Jeremiah that God's mercy to an unrepentant nation would not last forever. Human tendency assumes special privileges, whether deserved or not, will last forever.

LESSON 12

The Prophet Joel: The Battle Belongs to God

JESUS PROMISED US A future of wars and rumors of war.[1] Greed or perceived wrongs often incite the hearts of aggressors. Fear or outrage lodge in the hearts of defenders. People long for peace, but it eludes them.

Question: Is peace possible in this world? Explain.

The Valley of Jehoshaphat

This battle took place sometime during the reign of Jehoshaphat (872–848 BC).[2]

READ 2 CHR 20:1–13

1. Who were the aggressors in this story?

2. What was Jehoshaphat's first reaction?

3. What did Jehoshaphat complain about to God?

---

1. Matt 24:6.
2. Maas, "A Chronology of Bible Events and World Events," 598.

God's Unfolding Story of Salvation

READ DEUT 2:1–6, 9, 18, 19

4. Why did God protect Judah's enemies?

READ 2 CHR 20:14–30

5. What did God tell Jehoshaphat to do?

6. How did Jehoshaphat demonstrate his faith in God?

7. Who won the battle? Why?

8. How did they win the battle?

9. What was the result of this battle?

Joel: Two Sides to God's Judgment

Date of ministry: about 835–796 BC.[3] Joel finished prophesying seventy-four years before the fall of Israel, 210 years before the fall of Jerusalem, and 258 years before the edict of Cyrus, which allowed the Israelites to return to their land.[4] Joel lived in Judah and prophesied to the people of Judah.

---

3. Ibid., 1526.
4. Kendall, *A Tale of Two Kingdoms*, 145.

The Prophet Joel: The Battle Belongs to God

READ JOEL 2: 28–32; ACTS 2:1–21

1. What did the believers see and hear on the day of Pentecost?

2. What happened after the crowd gathered around the believers?

3. When was the primary fulfillment of Joel's prophecy?

4. What happens to those who call on the name of the Lord?

READ JOEL 2:32; REV 11:13

5. What will the survivors in Jerusalem do?

6. Explain why this is another fulfillment of Joel's prophecy.

READ JOEL 3:1–8; PS 126

7. What did God promise would happen to Judah's enemies?

8. What happened when God returned his people to the Promised Land?

9. Why did God call that time, the Valley of Jehoshaphat?

God's Unfolding Story of Salvation

READ JOEL 3:9–16; MATT 13:24–30, 36–43

10. Who will Jesus judge at the end of the world?

11. What will happen to the wicked and the righteous?

12. How will this final day be like the Valley of Jehoshaphat?

READ JOEL 3:17–21; REV 22:1–5

13. Compare these two passages.

Application: The Old Testament points to Jesus through preparation for his birth, direct prophecy, pictures or types, and anticipation. Which of these apply in this lesson?

Reflection: Whose side are you on? The sovereign God promises to fight and win the battle for believers.

Summary

On the day of Pentecost, the Holy Spirit opened the floodgates of revival. Thousands repented of their sins and trusted Jesus for their salvation. Others who rejected God died in unbelief. Similar revivals have occurred throughout history. In Revelation, John alludes to a revival among the residents of Jerusalem near the end of time.

In the Valley of Jehoshaphat, God reminded his people that the battle belongs to him. Since God is sovereign, no one can thwart his plans. In fact, those who trust him do not need to fight. Instead the Lord goes ahead, fights for believers, and accomplishes his will.

Joel also reminded the people of Judah that there are two sides to God's judgment. The Israelites would survive captivity and return to their own land. But the Lord would punish other nations for their treatment of his people. Likewise, at the end of time, some will receive eternal punishment while others will enjoy life, forever with God in a sin-free world.

Lesson 13

The Prophets Amos and Hosea: Loving the Unlovely

SOME HABITS ARE GOOD while others are bad. Sadly, we often act without thinking about the consequences. All habits are hard to break. Even good habits are dangerous, if our heart is not in it, for we end up becoming hypocrites.

Question: Why do people go to church?

Amos: Rejecting Ritualistic Religion

Date of ministry: about 760–750 BC.[1] Amos finished prophesying twenty-eight years before the fall of Israel and 212 years before the edict of Cyrus.[2]

READ AMOS 2:6–8; AMOS 5:7, 10–12

1. Amos came from Judah to warn Israel of its sins. What sins were the Israelites committing?

---

[1] Maas, "A Chronology of Bible Events and World Events," 1536.
[2] Kendall, *A Tale of Two Kingdoms*, 121.

READ AMOS 5:14, 15

2. What did God plead with Israel to do?

READ AMOS 7:10–13

3. What happened to Amos after he preached to the Israelites?

READ AMOS 4:4, 5; AMOS 6:1

4. How did the Israelites feel about their worship of God?

READ AMOS 5:21–23

5. How did God react to their worship?

READ AMOS 5:26–27; AMOS 7:9, 17

6. What would be the consequence of Israel's idolatry?

READ AMOS 1:3–15; AMOS 9:7–10, 13–15

7. How was Israel's punishment different from that of other nations?

READ 1 CHR 16:1–4

8. How did the Israelites worship God in David's tent?

God's Unfolding Story of Salvation

READ AMOS 9:11, 12; ACTS 15:1–6, 12–19

9. When did God restore David's fallen tent?

10. Who were the worshipers in the restored tent?

Hosea: The Love of God

Date of ministry: 753–715 BC.[3] Hosea prophesied for thirty-one years before the fall of Israel and for seven years afterward. He finished prophesying 177 years before the edict of Cyrus.[4] He is the only prophet of God to live in the northern kingdom of Israel and also write a book.

READ HOS 4:1, 2

1. What sins were the Israelites guilty of committing?

READ HOS 14:1, 2

2. What did God ask them to do?

READ HOS 8:1–3; HOS 10:5–8

3. What would happen to Israel?

---

3 Maas, "A Chronology of Bible Events and World Events," 1502.
4 Kendall, *A Tale of Two Kingdoms*, 126.

The Prophets Amos and Hosea: Loving the Unlovely

READ HOS 1:2, 3, 6–9

4. What do the names Lo-Ruhamah and Lo-Ammi mean?

READ HOS 1:10—2:1, 23

5. What did God promise Israel and Judah?

READ EZRA 1:1–4; ACTS 2:5

6. What was Cyrus' proclamation?

7. How did God keep his promise in the physical world?

READ ROM 9:22–26; ROM 10:12, 13

8. How did God fulfill this prophecy in the spiritual realm?

READ HOS 3:1–5

9. Why did God tell Hosea to take Gomer back?

10. How is Gomer a picture of Israel?

READ ACTS 2:36–41

11. How did the people respond to Peter's sermon?

God's Unfolding Story of Salvation

12. What were Peter's instructions to them?

Application: The Old Testament points to Jesus through preparation for his birth, direct prophecy, pictures or types, and anticipation. Which of these apply in this lesson?

Reflection: God continues to love hypocrites and idolaters. How can you show love to those unwilling to respond to you?

Summary

The Israelites were self-satisfied and pleased with their worship of God. They only appeared to worship, however. Their hearts were actually far from God. Through Amos, the Lord urged them to repent of their sin. Nevertheless, although judgment would fall on other nations permanently, God promised Israel that their punishment for not repenting would be short-lived.

In contrast to this hypocritical ritualistic worship, God looked forward to the New Testament era when Jew and Gentile would worship together in spirit and in truth. God would restore David's fallen tent when both groups would unite together for worship in the church. At this point in redemptive history, such a union was inconceivable to the Israelite mindset. After all, they were God's special people, not the other nations.

When they did not heed Amos' message, God sent Hosea to preach to the people. The Lord used Hosea's marriage to a prostitute as an object lesson on spiritual realities. Hosea became a picture of God's long-suffering love toward unrepentant sinners. Like Gomer, Israel did not deserve for the Lord to love her and treat her like a precious wife. True, God would restore them to their land after the captivity was over. Yet spiritual restoration was much more important to God than physical concerns. That is why the Lord reminded them of his covenant with David. On the day of Pentecost, many Israelites did indeed seek God and David their king, meaning Jesus. Therefore the Lord forgave three thousand people of their sins and saved them. The church was born.

Lesson 14

The Prophet Micah: Waiting for the Messiah

Date of ministry: 742–687 BC.[1]

MICAH PROPHESIED FOR TWENTY years before the fall of Israel and for thirty-five years afterward. He finished prophesying 101 years before the fall of Jerusalem and 149 years before the edict of Cyrus. Micah is primarily a prophet of Judah and the contemporary of Isaiah. He is one of only three prophets who wrote directly to Israel.[2]

I enjoy planning vacations with my family. We always try to cram as much into every day as we possibly can. I wait with eager anticipation for the day when the trip will begin.

Question: What events have you looked forward to in your life?

READ MIC 1:3–7; MIC 2:1–5

1. Micah warned Judah and Israel to repent. What sins were the Israelites guilty of committing?

2. What did God promise would happen to the disobedient nation?

---

1. Maas, "A Chronology of Bible Events and World Events," 1566.
2. Kendall, *A Tale of Two Kingdoms*, 130.

READ MIC 2:6, 7

3. How did the false prophets react to Micah's warnings?

READ MIC 2:12; MIC 7:8–12

4. What did God promise Israel in these verses?

READ NEH 1:1–4; NEH 12:27–30

5. How did God keep his promise to Israel?

READ MIC 7:18, 19; COL 2:13; 1 JOHN 1:8–10

6. Whose sins will God forgive?

7. What happens when God hurls all our iniquities into the depths of the sea?

READ MIC 5:2

8. Where would the Messiah be born?

READ LUKE 2:1–7

9. How did Jesus come to be born in Bethlehem?

God's Unfolding Story of Salvation

READ MIC 4:1, 2

10. What did God promise would happen?

READ LUKE 24:45–48; ACTS 2:5, 14–18

11. How was the prophecy in Micah fulfilled?

12. When are the last days?

READ MIC 4:3, 4; EPH 1:19–23; COL 1:3–6, 21–23

13. What power does Jesus have because of his death and resurrection?

14. How easily did the Gospel spread throughout the known world?

15. What gospel did Paul preach to everyone?

READ ACTS 2:42–47

16. What was life like for those first believers?

READ MIC 4:5

17. How many religions would there be during the Messiah's day?

The Prophet Micah: Waiting for the Messiah

READ MIC 4:6, 7; LUKE 7:18–23

18. How did Jesus prove he was the Messiah?

Application: The Old Testament points to Jesus through preparation for his birth, direct prophecy, pictures or types, and anticipation. Which of these apply in this lesson?

Reflection: How do you behave while you wait for God to answer your prayer requests?

Summary

After God made his covenant with David, the Israelites looked forward to a political king. Because the Hebrew language does not have one word denoting a king who has been anointed, the Israelites did not use the word "Messiah" until they learned Aramaic in Babylon.[3]

God entrusted Micah with detailed information on the coming King. Jesus would be born in Bethlehem, the birthplace of David. Unlike the political ruler expected by the Jews, Micah prophesied about a spiritual king and his effect on the world. Furthermore the Messiah would prove who he was by his miracles. Although false religions would continue to exist, the one true religion would spread quickly throughout the world. Following Jesus' death and resurrection, the Gospel did spread quickly through the Roman Empire. Before the cross only a few believed. Afterward the church grew exponentially.

Although God's people waited 700 years before Micah's prophecies came true, he turned out to be a reliable prophet of God. This should give us confidence to trust other promises of God in this book. Does God have the ability to forgive sin?

---

3. Wallace, "Messiah," 710.

Lesson 15

The Prophet Isaiah: Our Greatest Need, Spiritual Salvation

Date of ministry: 740–681 BC.[1]

ISAIAH BEGAN PROPHESYING EIGHTEEN years before the fall of Israel, 154 years before the fall of Jerusalem, and 202 years before the edict of Cyrus. While the Lord was blessing the northern kingdom of Israel during the reign of Jeroboam II (2 Kgs 14:25), he also was providing material prosperity to the southern kingdom of Judah.[2]

Reign of Uzziah (Azariah): 792–740 BC[3]

When my daughter Debra was in high school, she often came home for lunch. Usually I was so engrossed in playing the piano that I never heard her enter the house. She would tiptoe toward the living room and whisper, "Surprise!" For a split second, she would frighten me.

Question: How do you react to unexpected occurrences?

---

1. Maas, "A Chronology of Bible Events and World Events," 600.
2. Kendall, A Tale of Two Kingdoms, 152.
3. Maas, "A Chronology of Bible Events and World Events," 599.

Isaiah's Call

READ ISA 6:1–7

1. How did Isaiah react to the holiness and glory of God?

2. What did God do for Isaiah?

ISA 6:8–10; JOHN 12:37–43; HEB 3:12, 13

3. Why are the spiritual eyes of nonbelievers blind?

4. What factors contribute to hardness of heart?

READ ISA 1:18–20

5. How does God teach sinners their need of the Savior?

Immanuel, 732 BC[4]
Reign of Ahaz: 740–724 BC[5]

READ ISA 7:1–12

1. Why did God offer to give Ahaz a sign?

2. How did Ahaz react?

---

4. Price et al., "Synchronous History of the Nations," 256.
5. Fausset, Fausset's Bible Dictionary, 24.

God's Unfolding Story of Salvation

READ ISA 7:13–17; ISA 8:3, 4

3. What sign did God give Ahaz?

4. What was the primary fulfillment of this prophecy?

READ 2 KGS 16:5–9

5. On whom did Ahaz rely to save Judah from its enemies?

READ MATT 1:18–25

6. What was the secondary but more important fulfillment?

7. What does the word "Immanuel" mean?

READ ISA 9:6, 7; LUKE 1:30–33

8. Who would fulfill God's covenant with David?

9. How long will Jesus' kingdom last?

READ ISA 11:1, 10; ROM 15:7–12

10. Who is the Root of Jesse?

The Prophet Isaiah: Our Greatest Need, Spiritual Salvation

READ ISA 11:10; JOHN 12:30–33

11. How does Jesus draw people to God?

READ ISA 35:3–6; LUKE 7:20–23

12. What is the proof that Jesus is the Messiah?

13. Describe the character of Jesus by completing the chart.

Isa 11:2–5	New Testament	Fulfillment
Isa 11:2	Matt 3:16, 17 Luke 2:52	
Isa 11:3	John 7:21–24 John 2:24, 25	
Isa 11:4	Rev 19:11 Rev 19:15	
Isa 11:5	1 John 2:1 Heb 3:6	

Application: The Old Testament points to Jesus through preparation for his birth, direct prophecy, pictures or types, and anticipation. Which of these apply in this lesson?

Reflection: Isaiah looked forward to spiritual salvation from sin. This is our greatest need also. The long-awaited king would suffer and die for sinners. Do you believe this?

Summary

Isaiah's name means "the salvation of Jehovah,"[6] and his book deals with the same topic. Confronted with the holiness and glory of God, Isaiah collapsed in fear. Likewise, unless we recognize our sinful rebellion against God Almighty, we will not understand our need for the Savior. Afterward the Holy Spirit will continue to reason with us and draw us with the cords of love into his kingdom.

Through Isaiah, God teaches us that he keeps all his promises, whether short or long term. Shortly after the Lord had offered Ahaz a sign, the Assyrians conquered Damascus. Within four years they conquered and annexed all of Israel east of the Jordan River.[7] Thus God kept his promise.

Furthermore, over 700 years before Jesus' birth, God promised Isaiah that a virgin would conceive and bear a son, who would be fully God and fully man. This child would be the king promised by God in his covenant with David. The promised seed would rule with righteousness and faithfulness. As God the Son, he would have the ability to see into hearts and judge inner thoughts and motives. He would also prove he was the long-awaited Messiah by his miracles.

---

6. Ibid., 312.

7 Price et al., "Synchronous History of the Nations," 256.

Lesson 16

The Prophet Isaiah: Jesus, Mighty to Save

Date of ministry: 740–681 BC[1]

ONCE I SPENT A lot of time organizing picture albums, especially those of my parents and in-laws. I admired their baby pictures, but sometimes I could not recognize the features of the elderly person in the child's face.

Question: What common problem plagues humanity?

READ ISA 25:7, 8; ISA 26:19; 1 COR 15:50–57

1. Why do people die?

2. What does God promise believers?

3. Compare the present body of believers with their future one.

4. How did God conquer death and accomplish the salvation of believers?

---

1. Maas, "A Chronology of Bible Events and World Events," 600.

God's Unfolding Story of Salvation

READ ISA 63:1–6;[2] EPH 1:7, 8

5. Who is mighty to save?

READ MATT 27:46; JOHN 12:27–31

6. Who helped Jesus while he was on the cross?

7. Who did Jesus overcome on the cross?

READ REV 19:15–21

8. What did Jesus promise to do at the end of time?

READ ROM 5:9–11

9. What did Jesus accomplish on the cross?

10. How did Jesus fulfill or explain these Scriptures?

Isaiah 53	New Testament	Fulfillment/Explanation
Isa 53:1	John 12:37, 38 Rom 10:16	
Isa 53:3	Matt 16:21 Matt 27:27–31	
Isa 53:4	Matt 8:16, 17	

2. The primary fulfillment of this prophecy is the destruction of Edom. For the purpose of this study I shall concentrate on secondary but more important fulfillments.

Isa 53:5	John 19:33–37	
	Rom 5:1, 2	
Isa 53:6	Rom 4:25	
Isa 53:7	Mark 14:60, 61	
Isa 53:7, 8	Acts 8:26–35	
Isa 53:9	Matt 27:57–60	
	1 Pet 2:21–23	
Isa 53:12	Mark 15:27	
	Luke 22:37	

READ ISA 55:1, 2, 6, 7

11. What does God offer us in these verses?

12. Who may receive God's gift of salvation?

READ ISA 61:1–3; LUKE 4:16–21

13. What good news did Jesus proclaim?

READ MATT 9:13; LUKE 19:10

14. Who heard and accepted this good news?

READ ISA 11:6–9; ISA 65:17–19

15. What kind of world did Isaiah describe in these verses?

God's Unfolding Story of Salvation

READ ISA 24:5, 6

16. What kind of world do we live in?

READ ISA 60:11, 18–21; REV 21:22–27

17. Compare these two passages.

Application: The Old Testament points to Jesus through preparation for his birth, direct prophecy, pictures or types, and anticipation. Which of these apply in this lesson?

Reflection: Do you believe Jesus shed his blood on the cross to pay the penalty for your sins?

Summary

The Holy Spirit revealed an amazing amount of detail about Jesus' death over 700 years before it happened. In so doing, God proved he always keeps his promises. Therefore we can count on Jesus being mighty to save those who trust in him. We can also count on God ushering in the new heaven and new earth, a world free of sin, forever.

Lesson 17

The Prophets Zephaniah and Habakkuk: Persevering Faith

MANY PEOPLE THINK WORLDLY kingdoms and economic systems are invincible. After the great depression of the 1930s, no one thought it would ever happen again. Yet in the fall of 2008, economic chaos spread worldwide. Nothing lasts forever in this sin-torn world.

Question: What have you lost which appeared long lasting and secure?

Zephaniah: Mighty to Save

Date of ministry: 640–621 BC.[1]

Zephaniah finished prophesying thirty-five years before the fall of Jerusalem and eighty-three years before the edict of Cyrus.[2]

READ ZEPH 1:4–9, 14–18

1. What would soon happen to Judah?

---

1. Maas, "A Chronology of Bible Events and World Events,"1594.
2. Kendall, *A Tale of Two Kingdoms*, 181.

READ ZEPH 1:2, 3, 18

2. What will happen at the end of the world?

READ ZEPH 2:3

3. What advice did God give them? Why?

READ ZEPH 2:9–15

4. What would happen to other countries?

READ ZEPH 3:6–8, 13–17, 20; JER 29:10, 14

5. How would God prove he is mighty to save Judah?

6. How do these prophecies describe the end of the world?

Habakkuk: Living by Faith

Date of ministry: 612–589 BC.[3]

Habakkuk finished prophesying three years before the fall of Jerusalem and fifty-one years before the edict of Cyrus.[4]

READ HAB 1:2–6

1. What was Habakkuk's problem?

---

3. Maas, "A Chronology of Bible Events and World Events," 1587.
4. Kendall, *A Tale of Two Kingdoms*, 191.

2. How did God answer him?

READ HAB 1:13, 14

3. How did Habakkuk respond to God's answer?

READ HAB 2:2–8

4. What would eventually happen to the Babylonians?

5. How did God expect Habakkuk to live? Why?

READ ROM 1:16, 17; GAL 3:11

6. How does God make believers righteous?

7. Who may become a believer?

READ HEB 10:35–39

8. What is the will of God for a believer?

9. What is a believer's hope?

God's Unfolding Story of Salvation

READ HAB 2:14; PS 126:1–3

10. What did other nations acknowledge when the children of Judah returned from captivity?

11. What condition must exist before the final fulfillment of this verse?

READ HAB 2:20—3:7

12. How did God reveal his sovereignty?

13. How did Habakkuk react to God's power?

READ HAB 3:16–19

14. How did Habakkuk feel knowing the Babylonians would conquer Judah?

15. How did he demonstrate his faith in God?

Application: The Old Testament points to Jesus through preparation for his birth, direct prophecy, pictures or types, and anticipation. Which of these apply in this lesson?

Reflection: Does your faith remain strong in God during trials or does it waver?

Summary

Judah would soon experience horrendous suffering because of the Babylonians. Yet they could claim God's promise to restore them to their land. When it happened, God proved that he is mighty to save. Nevertheless spiritual salvation is much more important to the Lord.

Knowing the righteous would suffer as well as the wicked upset Habakkuk. But he still exhibited persevering faith. Although Habakkuk trembled as he thought about the future, he trusted in the sovereign God to care for him.

Lesson 18

The Prophet Jeremiah: A Circumcised Heart

Date of ministry: 627–586 BC.[1]

JEREMIAH PROPHESIED FOR FORTY-ONE years before the fall of Jerusalem and for a short time afterward. He finished prophesying forty-eight years before the edict of Cyrus.[2]

Life abounds with defining moments: graduation day, wedding day, a new job, or the death of a loved one. On New Year's Eve we celebrate the beginning of a new year. Everyone deals with change differently.

Question: How easily do you accept change in your life?

The Old Covenant

READ JER 11:2–5

1. What conditions does God require in this covenant?

READ JER 5:19; JER 30:4–7

2. What would happen to the children of Judah? Why?

---

1. Maas, "A Chronology of Bible Events and World Events," 1283.
2. Kendall, *A Tale of Two Kingdoms*, 183.

The Prophet Jeremiah: A Circumcised Heart

READ JER 29:10; JER 30:1–3; JER 33:10, 11

3. What sure hope did the children of Judah have?

READ EZRA 1:1–4

4. When did God keep his promise?

The Covenant with David

READ JER 23:5, 6; JER 30:8, 9; JER 33:14–16

1. Describe the characteristics of the coming king and his kingdom.

READ 2 SAM 7:12, 13; LUKE 1:30–33; MATT 2:1–6; JOHN 1:49

2. Who is the fulfillment of God's covenant with David?

READ HEB 1:3, 8; 2 PET 1:11

3. Where is Jesus' throne?

4. How long will Jesus' reign last?

READ REV 5:1–10

5. How did Jesus earn the right to become king?

6. When did his reign begin?

READ ISA 52:7

7. What is the central message of the kingdom?

The New Covenant

READ JER 31:27–30; DEUT 24:16; GAL 6:7, 8

1. Whose sin are you responsible for?

READ EXOD 20:5, 6

2. Explain the relationship between the sins of fathers and those of their children.

READ JER 31:31–34; HEB 8:6–13

3. Contrast the old and new covenants.

The Prophet Jeremiah: A Circumcised Heart

READ LUKE 22:20; 1 COR 11:25, 26

4. Whose blood was shed to ratify, or guarantee, the fulfillment of the new covenant?

READ JER 31:35, 36; ROM 9:6–8; ROM 11:1–6

5. Between AD 70 and 1948 there was no physical nation of Israel on earth. What kind of nation was God talking about? Explain how God told the truth in these verses.

READ ISA 66:8; ACTS 2:36–41

6. What happened on the day of Pentecost?

7. Who may belong to the spiritual nation of Israel?

READ JER 4:4; ROM 2:28, 29; PHIL 3:2, 3; COL 2:11

8. Who circumcises our hearts?

9. What does circumcision of the heart mean?

Application: The Old Testament points to Jesus through preparation for his birth, direct prophecy, pictures or types, and anticipation. Which of these apply in this lesson?

Reflection: "Since, then, you have been raised with Christ, set your hearts on things above, where Christ is, seated at the right hand of God. Set your minds on things above, not on earthly things" (Col 3:1–2). What are your priorities? Do you show by your priorities that God has circumcised your heart?

Summary

Jeremiah lived during the darkest period in Judah's history. Refusing to heed Jeremiah, his countrymen preferred false prophets to the word of God. Therefore they imprisoned him for warning them of the coming captivity. Eventually they threw him into a muddy cistern underneath the courtyard of the guard. But the king ordered thirty men to pull him out and rescue him from certain death (Jer 38:1–13).

In the midst of such difficult times, God promised Jeremiah a new covenant. The Lord would change the hearts of his people so that everyone would willingly love and obey him. He would even forgive their sins, forever. In the New Testament we learn why the new covenant replaced the old covenant. We also learn how the blood of Jesus guaranteed its fulfillment. Because of Jesus' death and resurrection, God inaugurated the everlasting covenant promised to David. In addition, Jesus earned the right to become king forever over a new community of believers, the church.

Lesson 19

The Prophet Ezekiel: The Holy Spirit, Living Water

Date of ministry: 593–571 BC.[1]

Ezekiel prophesied to the exiles for seven years before the fall of Jerusalem. His ministry ended thirty-three years before the edict of Cyrus.[2]

Most of my life I have been a stay-at-home mom. I enjoyed the opportunity and privilege of taking care of my family without the pressure of an outside job. Therefore it was quite a surprise when a friend once expressed concern over my spending so much time home alone. I wonder if some women feel like captives in their homes. I never did.

Question: Have you ever felt like a captive?

Life in Babylon

READ JER 29:1–11

1. How long would the people of Judah live in exile?

2. What were they to do in Babylon?

---

1. Maas, "A Chronology of Bible Events and World Events," 1399.
2. Kendall, *A Tale of Two Kingdoms*, 204.

Hope for the Future

READ EZEK 18:1–4, 20

1. Why was Ezekiel upset?

2. Whose sin are you responsible for?

READ EZEK 18:31, 32; EZEK 36:24–28

3. What did God ask the exiles to do?

4. What did God promise them?

READ EZEK 33:21–29

5. What mistaken ideas did the people of Judah hold?

6. Why were they wrong?

READ EZEK 37:1–10

7. What happened to the dead bones?

READ EPH 2:1, 2, 6, 7

8. How does God demonstrate his sovereignty in the spiritual realm?

READ EZEK 37:11–14, 21, 22; ACTS 2:5

9. How did God demonstrate his sovereignty in the physical world?

READ EZEK 37:24; EZEK 34:11–16; JOHN 10:7–18

10. What did God promise Ezekiel?

11. How is Jesus the fulfillment of this prophecy?

READ EZEK 37:25–28; REV 21:1–4

12. Compare the promises in Ezekiel with those in Revelation.

READ EZEK 43:9–11

13. What did God want the exiles to do after they had returned to Judah?

READ EZEK 44:9; HEB 12:22–24

14. Who belongs in God's sanctuary?

READ EZEK 47:1–5; JOHN 7:37–39

15. Describe what happened to the water under the temple.

16. Who does the water symbolize?

God's Unfolding Story of Salvation

READ ACTS 2:1–4, 40, 41

17. How many people did God save on the day of Pentecost?

18. Compare the effectiveness of the Holy Spirit before and after the day of Pentecost.

READ EZEK 47:12; REV 22:1, 2

19. Compare these two passages.

Application: The Old Testament points to Jesus through preparation for his birth, direct prophecy, pictures or types, and anticipation. Which of these apply in this lesson?

Reflection: How is the Holy Spirit working in your life?

Summary

Life was very different for the captives in Babylon from those in Egypt many years before. The Babylonians did not treat them like slaves or conscript them into forced labor. Nevertheless they were sad, discouraged, and homesick. How they missed worshiping at the temple!

    For seven years Ezekiel warned the children of Judah that the Babylonians would conquer Jerusalem. But they refused to believe God would allow it. Moreover they often blamed their forefathers for their predicament. Ezekiel objected by insisting each person must take responsibility for his or her own sin.

The Prophet Ezekiel: The Holy Spirit, Living Water

Like Isaiah and Jeremiah, Ezekiel prophesied God would restore his people to the Promised Land. The Lord used this physical restoration as an object lesson to prove his ability to provide spiritual reconciliation to individuals. For years most of the people had failed to love and obey God. Now God would circumcise their hearts so that obedience would be internal, not external. No longer would they worship God outwardly and not mean it.

While Ezekiel was stuck in a foreign land, the Lord offered him spiritual hope for the future. Ezekiel could look forward to the day when the Messiah as the shepherd king would watch over his people. No earthly king ever acted like a shepherd leading his people to green pastures and cool water. Rather they were despots, demanding obedience and exacting punishment for disobedience. In the New Testament, Jesus is the Good Shepherd protecting his flock, the church.

Ezekiel also saw the influence of the Holy Spirit starting out like a tiny stream from Jerusalem. Eventually his influence would spread throughout the world and become an impassable river. The New Testament records the fulfillment of Ezekiel's prophecies. After Pentecost, thousands believed Jesus took the punishment, which they deserved. They repented of their sin and trusted in the finished work of Jesus on Calvary to restore them to fellowship with God. Because the Holy Spirit spread this Gospel, God has changed the hearts of people worldwide. Thus Ezekiel shows how the Holy Spirit works in history to fulfill God's plans.

Ezekiel ends his book with a vision similar to the city of God in Revelation 22. Since God told the truth so far, we can count on him completing his plans.

Lesson 20

The Prophet Daniel: Living by Faith, Not by Sight

Date of ministry: 605–536 BC.[1]

DANIEL FINISHED PROPHESYING TWO years after the edict of Cyrus and 361 years before Antiochus Epiphanes began to reign.[2]

Antiochus Epiphanes, king of the Seleucid Empire: 175–164 BC[3]

When two companies consider merging, delegates from each one meet secretly to discuss a deal. If the negotiators agree on the terms of the merger, each company will approach its investors. If they approve, the companies will inform their staff. Everyone finds out on a need-to-know basis. I wonder why God revealed his plans to Nebuchadnezzar, a heathen emperor.

Question: What have you learned about after the fact?

READ DAN 2:1–6, 24–45

1. Compare earthly kingdoms to God's kingdom.

2. When did God promise to set up his kingdom?

---

1. Maas, "A Chronology of Bible Events and World Events," 1473.
2. Kendall, *A Tale of Two Kingdoms*, 219.
3. Price et al., "Synchronous History of the Nations," 266.

The Prophet Daniel: Living by Faith, Not by Sight

READ MARK 1:14, 15

3. What good news did Jesus proclaim?

READ MATT 16:17–20

4. What is the relationship between the church and God's kingdom?

READ DAN 7:1–14; EPH 1:19–23; REV 5:1–10

5. Who are the Ancient of Days and the Son of Man?

6. When did the Son of Man receive authority over every living creature?

7. How long will the Son of Man's kingdom last?

READ DAN 7:8, 21, 22; DAN 8:21–25

8. Why do you think God told Daniel about the little horn?

READ DAN 7:25–28

9. What does the expression "time, times, and half a time" teach us about the length of tribulation?

READ DAN 6:1–28

10. What persecution did Daniel endure?

God's Unfolding Story of Salvation

11. Daniel's faith in God remained strong in spite of persecution. What was the result?

READ DAN 9:25; NEH 1:1–4; NEH 2:4–6

12. How many years before the Anointed One would come? (Seven means seven years.)

13. How did God keep his promise to rebuild Jerusalem after the captivity was over?

READ DAN 9:26, 27; 1 COR 1:23–26; HEB 10:11–18

14. What did God mean when he said the Anointed One would be cut off?

15. What covenant put an end to the sacrificial system forever?

16. Why did God allow Titus, the Roman commander, to conquer Jerusalem and destroy the temple in AD 70?

READ DAN 12:2, 3; MATT 25:46; 1 COR 15:50–54

17. What did God promise Daniel? Can we count on this also?

Application: The Old Testament points to Jesus through preparation for his birth, direct prophecy, pictures or types, and anticipation. Which of these apply in this lesson?

Reflection: Faith involves living day by day without knowledge of the future. We only know what God reveals in the Bible. How are you exercising your faith while waiting for Jesus' second coming?

Summary

God gave Daniel and Nebuchadnezzar an overview of history, but for different reasons. The powerful king of Babylon learned earthly kingdoms exist only with God's permission and do not last forever. In contrast, God's kingdom will never end. The four kingdoms in Nebuchadnezzar's dream turned out to be Babylon, Medo-Persia, Greece, and Rome. As promised, Jesus was born in the days of Caesar Augustus, emperor of Rome.

Daniel, on the other hand, found out trouble lay ahead. Moreover his vision of earthly kingdoms differed from Nebuchadnezzar's. Instead of a statue he saw wild animals. The leopard symbolized the Greek Empire. History records how generals fought to gain control of this empire after the death of Alexander the Great. Eventually they divided the empire into four separate kingdoms. Many years later the Seleucids of Syria wrestled Palestine from the Ptolemaic kings of Egypt. When the Seleucid king, Antiochus Epiphanes, desecrated the temple in 168 BC, those prophecies of persecution for God's people came true.

Daniel's vision of the Son of Man's coronation overshadowed this bad news. In addition, God revealed when the king would pay the penalty for sin. Thus ending the necessity of the sacrificial system set up by Moses.

Although troubled by his visions, Daniel trusted God to keep his promises. Like Daniel, believers should expect persecution. Like Daniel, believers can look forward to the resurrection of their bodies and God's eternal kingdom. Like Daniel, believers must live by faith in God and without complete knowledge of the future.

LESSON 21

The Prophets Haggai and Zechariah: Obeying God

My husband has made to-do lists for years. Seeing how he completed tasks around the house, because he was so organized, inspired me to try this also. I discovered one difficulty, however. Sometimes I keep moving certain jobs to the bottom of every new list. My underlying problem is procrastination.

Question: What tasks do you keep on avoiding?

The Edict of Cyrus, 538 BC[1]

READ EZRA 1:1–4

1. Why did Cyrus make this edict?

READ JER 25:11–14; JER 29:10–14

2. What did God promise Jeremiah?

READ EZRA 3:8–13

3. How did the people react when they saw the foundation of the new temple?

---

1. Price, et al., "Synchronous History of the Nations," 260.

The Prophets Haggai and Zechariah: Obeying God

READ EZRA 4:1–5, 24

4. Why did the people stop building the temple?

Haggai: Building the Temple

Date written: 520 BC.[2] Haggai prophesied eighteen years after the edict of Cyrus.[3]

Reign of Darius, king of Persia: 521–485 BC[4]

READ HAG 1:1–4

1. Why did God tell Zerubbabel and Joshua to build the temple?

READ HAG 1:5–11

2. Why were the people always struggling to survive?

READ HAG 1:12–15

3. How did the people respond to Haggai's message?

READ HAG 2:1–5

4. What does God say to encourage them to finish building the temple?

---

2. Maas, "A Chronology of Bible Events and World Events," 1603.
3. Kendall, A Tale of Two Kingdoms, 237.
4. Price, "Synchronous History of the Nations," 260.

God's Unfolding Story of Salvation

READ HAG 2:6–9; MATT 21:12

5. Who is the desired of all nations?

6. Why was this temple greater than Solomon's?

READ EZRA 6:16–18

7. What did they do as soon as they finished building the temple?

Zechariah: Waiting for the King

Chapters 1–8 written: about 520–518 BC. Chapters 9–14 written: about 480 BC.[5] Zechariah began to prophesy eighteen years after the edict of Cyrus.[6]

1. Complete the chart to see how Jesus fulfilled these prophesies in his first coming.

Zechariah	New Testament	Fulfillment
Zech 9:9	John 12:14, 15	
Zech 9:11	Matt 26:28	
Zech 13:7	Mark 14:27, 43–50	
Zech 11:12, 13	Matt 27:5–10	
Zech 12:10	John 19:34–37	
Zech 12:10	Acts 2:37–41	
Zech 13:1	1 John 1:7	

5. Maas, "A Chronology of Bible Events and World Events," 1608.
6. Kendall, A Tale of Two Kingdoms, 239.

The Prophets Haggai and Zechariah: Obeying God

READ ZECH 14:7–9; REV 1:7; REV 11:15; REV 22:1–5

2. What unique day do Zechariah and believers look forward to?

Application: The Old Testament points to Jesus through preparation for his birth, direct prophecy, pictures or types, and anticipation. Which of these apply in this lesson?

Reflection: God planned very carefully for Jesus' first coming. No matter what trouble Satan instigated, he could not foil God's plans. Will you trust the Lord to work in your life? Are you willing to obey him and do whatever task he assigns you?

Summary

Shortly after Cyrus, king of Persia, conquered the Babylonians, he decreed the exiles could return to Judah and rebuild their temple. After this time, no one prophesied about the Jew's restoration from captivity, for there was no need. Many Israelites returned home and joyfully began to build the foundation of the temple. Then fearing opposition from their neighbors, they stopped the work. When the temple remained unfinished eighteen years later, God used the prophets Zechariah and Haggai to encourage the people to finish building it. Over 500 years later, the promised seed would enter that temple and fulfill the prophecies concerning his first coming.

Lesson 22

The Prophets Malachi and John the Baptist: Witnessing for God

I HEARD SOME TERRIFYING sermons as a young girl. Those preachers did not hesitate to rebuke people for their sin. They pointed out the consequence of continued disobedience—eternity in hell.

Question: When was the last time you heard a sermon about the consequences of rejecting God?

Malachi: The Coming of the Lord

Date written: about 430 BC.[1]

Malachi prophesied 108 years after the edict of Cyrus, eighty-six years after the people had rebuilt the temple, twenty-eight years after Ezra had taught the people the law of God, and fifteen years after Nehemiah had built the walls.[2]

READ MAL 1:6–10

1. How were the priests showing disrespect for God?

---

1. Maas, "A Chronology of Bible Events and World Events," 1627.
2. Kendall, *A Tale of Two Kingdoms*, 252.

The Prophets Malachi and John the Baptist: Witnessing for God

2. How did God feel about this situation?

READ MAL 1:11; MATT 8:10, 11

3. Who will honor and worship God properly?

READ MAL 3:1; JOHN 1:23, 29, 30; LUKE 3:2, 3

4. Who was the messenger who would prepare the way?

5. What was his message?

6. Who is the messenger of the covenant?

READ MAL 3:2, 3; JOHN 2:13–16

7. How was Jesus like a refiner's fire?

READ MAL 4:1, 2; 2 PET 3:7

8. What two kinds of people are there?

9. What will happen at the end of the world?

John the Baptist: God's Messenger, AD 26[3]

READ MATT 3:1–6

1. Where did John preach?

2. Who came to hear him?

3. What was his message?

READ MATT 3:7–10

4. Why did John call the Pharisees and Sadducees a brood of vipers?

READ MATT 3:11, 12; ACTS 1:5; ACTS 2:1–4

5. Compare John's baptism with Jesus'.

READ MATT 3:13–17; 2 COR 5:21

6. Why did John refuse to baptize Jesus at first?

7. How did John baptizing Jesus fulfill all righteousness?

8. What happened as soon as John baptized him?

---

3. Maas, "A Chronology of Bible Events and World Events," 1723.

The Prophets Malachi and John the Baptist: Witnessing for God

READ JOHN 1:29–34; 1 PET 1:18–20

9. Why did John call Jesus, "the Lamb of God"?

10. Why did John baptize with water?

READ MAL 4:5, 6; MATT 11:7–15

11. What would be the effect of John's preaching?

READ MATT 14:3–5

12. Why did Herod arrest John?

READ JAS 5:17; REV 11:3–6

13. In what way are the two witnesses in Revelation like Elijah?

Application: The Old Testament points to Jesus through preparation for his birth, direct prophecy, pictures or types, and anticipation. Which of these apply in this lesson?

Reflection: Are you telling those around you about Jesus while you are waiting for his return?

Summary

Disgusted at the irreverent worship of the priests, Malachi looked forward to the messenger of the covenant, the desired of the nations, coming as a refiner's fire to cleanse the temple. God also promised to send another messenger ahead of the desired of the nations. This person would announce his arrival and prepare the hearts of the people. Over four hundred years passed before Malachi's prophecies came true. God chose John the Baptist to announce the coming of Jesus, the promised seed. After Herod had imprisoned John the Baptist, Jesus told a crowd that John was indeed the prophet Elijah promised by God in Malachi.

Malachi also looked forward to the time when God would burn up the world and punish evildoers. Then the righteous would rejoice. In Revelation 11, the apostle John prophesies about two witnesses with powers similar to Elijah. Therefore Malachi's prophecy of Elijah must have another fulfillment immediately before Jesus' second coming.

PART THREE

Jesus, the Promised Seed

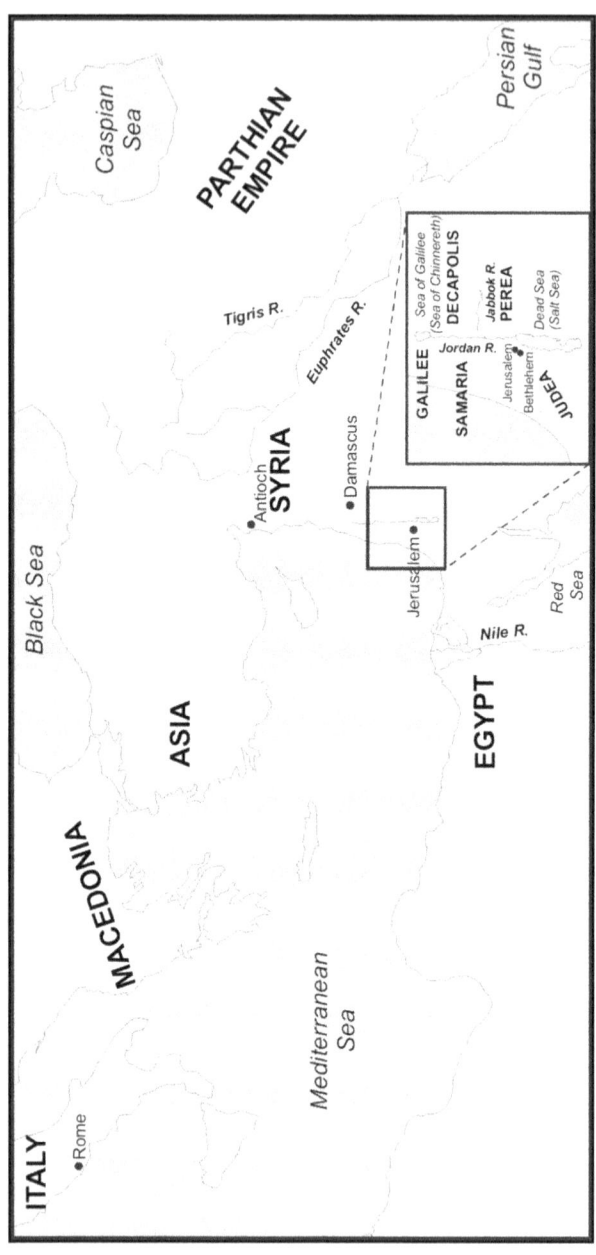

Figure 4: World of Jesus, the Promised Seed [1]

1. Kendall, *A Tale of Two Kingdoms*, 288.

LESSON 23

The Birth of the Promised Seed: Responding to Jesus

ONCE I WORKED FOR a company that went bankrupt. Although the store remained open for a few more weeks, employees needed to find new positions elsewhere. Many people have experienced similar unanticipated changes.

Question: What unexpected event disrupted your life?

Mary

READ LUKE 1:26–31

1. Why did the angel Gabriel visit Mary?

READ LUKE 1:32, 33

2. What did Gabriel tell Mary about Jesus?

READ LUKE 1:34–38

3. How did Mary react to Gabriel's news?

Joseph

READ MATT 1:18, 19

1. How did Joseph think he should solve his problem?

READ MATT 1:20–25

2. What did the angel command Joseph to do? Why?

3. What does Jesus' name mean?

4. What prophecy was God about to fulfill?

5. How did Joseph display his faith in God?

The Birth of Jesus, 6/5 BC[2]

READ LUKE 2:1–7; MIC 5:2

1. How did God fulfill his promise about the birthplace of Jesus?

READ LUKE 2:8–20

2. What good news did the shepherds hear?

---

2. Maas, "A Chronology of Bible Events and World Events," 1636.

The Birth of the Promised Seed: Responding to Jesus

3. How did the shepherds demonstrate their faith in God?

4. How did Mary react?

The Wise Men, 5/4 BC[3]

Reign of Herod the Great, king of Judea: 37–4 BC[4]

READ MATT 2:1, 2

1. Why did the wise men travel to Jerusalem?

2. What did they ask the inhabitants of Jerusalem?

READ MATT 2:3–6

3. What did the chief priests and teachers of the law tell them?

READ MATT 2:7–12

4. How did the wise men feel when they found Jesus?

5. What did they do?

---

3. Ibid., 1636.
4. Ibid., 1636.

READ MATT 2:13–18

6. How did Herod respond when the wise men did not return to Jerusalem?

Reflection: How are you responding to Jesus' birth?

Summary

Everyone must respond in some way to Jesus. Mary, Joseph, and the wise men rejoiced at Jesus' arrival. In contrast, the inhabitants of Jerusalem ignored news of his birth. Herod, on the other hand, tried to kill him. But God would not allow Satan to thwart his plan of salvation. Therefore he protected his Son from Herod's evil schemes.

Lesson 24

Jesus' Ministry: The Necessity of Spiritual Birth

AD 26/27–30[1]

My pastor once explained the difference between sympathy and compassion. A sympathetic person cares about someone else only on an intellectual level. Compassion reaches out and touches another person's world to help them. Before I began chemotherapy, my friend gave me a satin pillowcase to cushion my head at night during cancer treatment. This is compassion.

Question: Under what circumstances have you experienced the compassion of a friend?

Nicodemus

READ JOHN 3:1, 2

1. Why did Nicodemus visit Jesus at night?

READ JOHN 3:3, 4

2. Why was Nicodemus confused?

---

1. Maas, "A Chronology of Bible Events and World Events," 1637.

God's Unfolding Story of Salvation

READ JOHN 3:5–8

3. Who is the only one with the ability to make a person a member of God's kingdom?

4. What did Jesus teach Nicodemus about spiritual birth?

READ JOHN 3:9–15; NUM 21:8, 9

5. Why did Jesus chide Nicodemus?

6. What would happen to Jesus?

READ JOHN 3:16–21

7. What did God do?

8. What two kinds of people are there?

9. What is eternal life?

10. How may a person receive eternal life?

The Divinity of Jesus

READ JOHN 5:1–8

1. What was the invalid's problem?

2. How did Jesus respond?

READ JOHN 5:9–13

3. Why were the Jews so angry that the invalid could walk?

READ JOHN 5:14–15

4. What did Jesus warn the man when they met in the temple?

READ JOHN 5:16–18

5. What upset the Jews so much?

Reflection: Is Jesus your Lord and Savior?

Summary

Jesus proved his divinity whenever he performed miracles in this physical world. Then, on Calvary, Jesus took our place and sacrificed himself for sinners. Afterward the Holy Spirit began to move in hearts like the wind so that sinners would repent and trust in Jesus for their spiritual salvation.

Lesson 25

The Disciples of Jesus: Learning from the Master

JEALOUSY OR INSECURITY MAY lead people to have a combative attitude. They may be so out of control that their quarrelsome words do not make sense. Jesus had to deal with grumblers, upset with what he said.

Question: How do you deal with argumentative people?

Choosing His Disciples

READ MARK 1:14, 15

1. What good news did Jesus proclaim?

READ MATT 4:23–25; LUKE 6:17–19

2. How did the people respond to Jesus?

3. How did Jesus prove his reliability in the spiritual realm?

The Disciples of Jesus: Learning from the Master

READ MATT 5:1–12; LUKE 6:20–23

4. Describe the characteristics of the members of God's kingdom.

5. What are the spiritual benefits of belonging to God's kingdom?

6. Why should the disciples rejoice when persecuted?

READ MATT 6:28–34

7. What priorities does God expect his followers to have?

8. What does Jesus promise to those who obey?

READ MATT 7:24–27

9. Describe the two kinds of people mentioned here.

Driving out Demons

READ MATT 12:22–30

1. How did the Pharisees try to discredit Jesus?

2. What was wrong with their argument?

3. What did Jesus' miracle prove?

The Growth of the Kingdom

READ LUKE 13:18–20

1. How is God's kingdom like a mustard seed?

2. Compare God's kingdom with yeast.

A Clash Concerning the Kingdom

READ JOHN 6:1–13

1. What miracle did Jesus perform?

READ JOHN 6:14, 15

2. How did the people react to this miracle?

3. Knowing their intentions, what did Jesus do? Why?

The Disciples of Jesus: Learning from the Master

READ JOHN 6:22–27

4. Why did the people search for Jesus the next day?

5. What kind of food did Jesus offer them?

READ JOHN 6:28–36

6. What did Jesus ask the people to do?

7. What kind of bread did the people want?

8. What did Jesus offer instead?

9. Why did they have difficulty understanding him?

READ JOHN 6:37–40; ROM 9:19–23

10. Describe God's sovereignty in salvation.

READ JOHN 6:41, 42, 47–52, 60–66

11. Why did many of Jesus' followers reject his teaching?

Reflection: Even believers have blind spots. May the Holy Spirit open our eyes and correct our thinking. Let us pray we have priorities pleasing to the Lord.

Summary

Jesus had his work cut out for him. For one thousand years God's people had been waiting for the king promised to David. Most of them, including his disciples, expected a political messiah. But Jesus knew they had a more important need—spiritual salvation. Ever since Jesus had called his disciples, he only taught them about spiritual realities and a spiritual kingdom. That was why he clashed with society. People mistakenly assumed his miracles meant the inauguration of a political kingdom.

Lesson 26

Mistaken Ideas about Jesus: Discerning the Truth

People have many different ideas about who Jesus is. Sadly, they either do not know or else do not care what the Bible says. Truth is what counts.

Question: How do you react to mistaken ideas?

Peter's Confession

READ MATT 16:13–20

1. What were some ideas of who Jesus was?

2. What did Simon Peter believe about Jesus? Why?

3. What are two fundamental truths upon which Jesus founded his church?

READ JOHN 6:14, 15

4. After Peter's confession, why did Jesus warn his disciples not to tell others who he was?

READ JOHN 20:21–23

5. How does the church know what to commend and what to condemn?

READ MATT 18:15–20; ACTS 16:4, 5

6. What authority does the church have?

READ MATT 16:21–23

7. What would soon happen to Jesus?

8. How did Peter react?

9. Why did Jesus denounce Peter so soon after blessing him?

READ MATT 16:24–26; MARK 8:34–37

10. What is important to Jesus?

Mistaken Ideas about Jesus: Discerning the Truth

READ MATT 16:27, 28; MARK 8:38—9:1; ACTS 2:1–4

11. What will happen at Jesus' return?

12. How do you know if Jesus' kingdom came during the disciples' lifetime?

Abraham's Children

READ JOHN 8:31–41

1. How did Jesus offend some Jews?

2. Why did they want to kill Jesus?

3. How were they different from Abraham?

READ JOHN 8:42–47

4. Why did Jesus tell those Jews that the devil was their father?

5. How may one become a spiritual descendant of Abraham?

Reflection: Let us pray for wisdom to discern truth from error.

Summary

Genealogy was important to the Jews. For 1500 years they were God's special people. Moreover they traced their physical descent back to Abraham. Jesus collided with this thinking by caring more about Abraham's spiritual descendants—those who knew they were sinners in need of a Savior—than with physical heritage.

In addition to correcting false thinking, Jesus taught his disciples the foundational doctrines upon which he would build his church. Because of the formation of synagogues during the Babylonian captivity, Jesus' disciples were used to the idea of small groups of people meeting to worship God. Therefore the concept of "church" was not foreign to them.

Lesson 27

Jesus: Nearing the End—Submitting to the Father's Will

No one enjoys watching a loved one suffer from a debilitating illness. Some people travel across the ocean or long distances to find a cure for their sicknesses.

Question: Have you traveled far for medical treatment?

Lazarus

READ JOHN 11:1–3, 17–22

1. How long had Lazarus been dead before Jesus arrived?

2. Describe Martha's conflicting emotions.

READ JOHN 11:23–27

3. What kind of power did Jesus claim to have in the physical and spiritual realms?

4. What did Martha confess by faith?

READ JOHN 11:38–44

5. How did Jesus prove his reliability?

READ JOHN 11:45–53

6. Why did the chief priests and Pharisees call a meeting of the Sanhedrin (the Jewish high council)?

7. What did the high priest Caiphas decide?

8. Explain how God used their evil intentions for good.

9. What would Jesus' death accomplish for believing Jews and Gentiles?

The Nature of the Kingdom

READ LUKE 17:20, 21; JOHN 18:36, 37

1. Describe the kind of kingdom Jesus founded.

2. Why was Jesus born?

Jesus: Nearing the End—Submitting to the Father's Will

READ LUKE 19:10

3. What did Jesus accomplish on earth?

The Ambition of James and John

READ MATT 19:27–30; MARK 10:28–31

1. What did Peter complain about to Jesus?

READ 1 COR 6:1–3; MATT 25:31–34, 41

2. When is the renewal of all things?

3. What will happen at the renewal?

READ MARK 10:32–34; LUKE 18:31–34

4. Why did Jesus go to Jerusalem?

5. Why did the disciples not understand what Jesus said?

READ MARK 10:35–41

6. What did James and John want?

7. How did the other disciples react?

God's Unfolding Story of Salvation

READ MARK 10:42–45

8. What did Jesus teach them to correct their thinking?

Reflection: Let us ask for courage to carry out God's will no matter what the circumstances.

Summary

The Pharisees were teachers of the law, and the Sadducees were priests. Over time the Pharisees devised rules to guard the law. These rules were like a fence meant to keep the Jews from breaking God's law. When Jesus broke some of their rules, the Pharisees were very angry. Yet they could not hurt Jesus until the Sadducees wanted him dead. Lazarus was the catalyst uniting the two groups with a common deadly purpose.

When the Sanhedrin met, Caiphas had no idea how prophetic his words would be. He thought it was better for Jesus to die so that the nation could keep its status quo with Rome. In reality, Jesus chose to die in order to redeem a people for God.

At this point in time, the disciples did not understand the nature of Jesus' kingdom or that he would earn the right to reign by dying on a cruel cross. Submitting to the Father's will, Jesus began his last walk toward Jerusalem.

Lesson 28

The Last Week of Jesus' Ministry: A Faithful Servant

Crushed under the strong arm of Rome, the Jews longed for political autonomy. Instead Jesus healed the sick, made the blind to see, and raised the dead. News of Jesus riding on a donkey toward the city of Jerusalem excited the crowd. They hoped Jesus would be their political messiah and save them from Roman rule. That is why they shouted, "Hosanna!" meaning "Save!"[1]

Question: How did you feel the last time you were part of a crowd waiting for something special to happen?

Welcoming the King

Sunday of his last week[2]

READ MARK 11:1–3

1. What did Jesus ask two of his disciples to do?

2. What was special about the colt?

---

1. Mark 11:9, n.
2. Robertson, *A Harmony of the Gospels for Students of the Life of Christ*, 152.

READ MARK 11:4–10; MATT 21:6–11; LUKE 19:37, 38

3. How did the people celebrate Jesus' arrival to Jerusalem?

READ MARK 10:32–34

4. Compare the crowd's expectations with Jesus' purpose in going to Jerusalem.

The Mount of Olives Discourse

Tuesday afternoon of his last week[3]

READ MATT 24:1–3

1. What did Jesus predict would happen?

2. What did the disciples ask Jesus?

READ MATT 24:4–14

3. Birth pains gradually occur more often and increase in intensity. What circumstances did Jesus say would be like these?

READ MATT 24:32–34

4. The Roman army under Titus destroyed the temple in AD 70. How does this knowledge make you feel about Jesus' reliability?

3. Ibid., 173.

The Last Week of Jesus' Ministry: A Faithful Servant

READ MATT 24:36–44

5. What will life be like just before Jesus' second coming?

6. Who is the only one who knows when Jesus will return?

READ MATT 24:45–51

7. How should a believer spend his or her time?

READ MATT 25:1–13

8. What did the bridegroom say to the five foolish virgins?

9. Parables are fictional stories with spiritual meanings. Explain what this parable teaches about the opportunity for salvation after Jesus returns.

READ MATT 25:31–46

10. What standard will Jesus use to judge people?

11. What will happen to the sheep and the goats?

READ MATT 26:1–5

12. How do these verses show Jesus' sovereignty?

13. Why were the chief priests and elders responsible for their actions?

Mary of Bethany

Tuesday evening of his last week[4]

READ MATT 26:6–13; JOHN 12:2–8

1. What did Mary do?

2. How did Judas react?

3. What did Jesus think of Mary's actions?

READ MATT 26:14–16; LUKE 22:1–6

4. What did Judas do?

5. How did Judas intend to betray Jesus?

---

4. Ibid., 187.

Reflection: Are you spending time in God's word and then acting on it? The Lord calls us to be a faithful servant by trusting and obeying him.

Summary

Mary of Bethany loved to sit at Jesus' feet and listen to him. One evening she surprised everyone at dinner when she poured a jar of expensive perfume over Jesus' head. By her actions she proved she was a faithful and wise servant of the Lord. Likewise, God calls us to be faithful and wise servants.

Will Jesus find us busy in his work at his second coming? No one knows the day or the hour of his return. When he does come back, he will separate the sheep from the goats. Then no one will have a second chance to be saved.

Lesson 29

The Death of Jesus: Completing God's Plan

MANY YEARS AGO ROAD construction sites did not have electric lights to warn motorists at night. Instead they had kerosene lamps. One evening a young girl ran into one of those lamps and knocked it over. The lamp set her clothing on fire. As soon as one of my husband's cousins saw what had happened, he rolled the girl in the grass to put out the fire. In so doing, he burnt his hand.

Paul writes, "Very rarely will anyone die for a righteous man, though for a good man someone might possibly dare to die. But God demonstrates his own love for us in this: While we were still sinners, Christ died for us" (Rom 5:7, 8). Jesus went to the cross willingly to complete God's plan of salvation. No one forced him to die.

Question: Can you recount a story of one who risked his or her life for another?

The Upper Room

Thursday, the evening before Jesus' crucifixion[1]

READ LUKE 22:7–20

1. What two events did Jesus celebrate?

---

1. Robertson, *Harmony of the Gospels for Students of the life of Christ*, 190.

The Death of Jesus: Completing God's Plan

READ MATT 3:14, 15; MATT 5:17, 18; LUKE 16:16, 17

2. Why is the order in which he celebrated them important?

READ HEB 8:6–13

3. What is significant about the new covenant?

READ JOHN 13:21–30

4. Why did Judas leave?

READ JOHN 14:1–6

5. Who provides the only access to God the Father?

READ JOHN 14: 15–19

6. What did Jesus promise his disciples and us?

READ JOHN 14:26; JOHN 16:12–15

7. What will the Holy Spirit do for Jesus' disciples?

8. What will the Holy Spirit do for believers?

The Arrest of Jesus

Friday, long before dawn[2]

READ MARK 14:32–42

1. What did Jesus pray?

READ MARK 14:43–50; JOHN 18:1–8

2. How did Judas betray Jesus?

3. How did Jesus show he was in control of his arrest?

The Trial of Jesus

READ MARK 14:55–65

1. What was unfair about Jesus' trial?

2. How did Jesus behave when the witnesses gave their testimonies?

3. How did Jesus show he was in control of the trial's outcome?

4. What happened to Jesus after he was found guilty?

---

2. Ibid., 205.

The Death of Jesus: Completing God's Plan

READ MARK 15:1–15

5. Why did Pilate authorize Jesus' crucifixion?

The Significance of the Cross

READ 1 JOHN 4:9, 10; ROM 5:8–11; HEB 2:14, 15

1. Why did Jesus die?

READ ROM 3:21–26

2. How does Jesus' death demonstrate God's justice and mercy toward sinners?

3. How may a sinner become righteous in God's sight?

Reflection: Although no one could kill Jesus without his authorization, Judas and Caiphas must accept responsibility for their part. Ultimately each of us must accept responsibility for Jesus' death.

Summary

When something new happens, which we are not expecting, we are often slow to realize its significance. This is what happened to the disciples. After Moses had led the Israelites out of Egypt, God instructed them to celebrate the Passover annually. On the first day of the feast, Jesus directed Peter and John to prepare the Passover supper. That evening Jesus and his disciples gathered in a large upper room to remember how God had rescued the Israelites from Egypt and slavery.

During the meal Jesus told the disciples that he wanted to eat this Passover with them before he would suffer. As soon as they had finished the Passover meal, Jesus instituted a new covenant remembrance. Thus he prepared them for the transition from the old covenant to the new. At this point the disciples did not understand what had happened. They were unaware of the significance of Jesus' words or actions.

After they had finished eating, Jesus spent some time comforting his disciples and preparing them for what was about to happen. Knowing they would be heartbroken at his death, Jesus encouraged them to focus on the fact that he would come back someday. He promised to send the Holy Spirit, who would comfort them and enable them to recall all of Jesus' words. The Holy Spirit also teaches believers today by reminding us of God's words in the Bible and by helping us understand what we read.

Lesson 30

The Resurrection and Ascension: A Time for Rejoicing

THOSE WHO SUFFER A serious illness undergo a gamut of emotions. For me, reaching the end of cancer treatment was the light at the end of a dark tunnel.

Question: How did you feel in a tough situation?

Resurrection Sunday, AD 30[1]

READ LUKE 24:1–12

1. How did the women feel when they saw the empty tomb?

2. How did the men react to the women's news?

3. What did Peter think after he had been to the tomb?

---

1 Maas, "A Chronology of Bible Events and World Events," 1867.

God's Unfolding Story of Salvation

READ LUKE 24:13–24

4. Why were Cleopas and his friend sad?

READ LUKE 24:25–35

5. What new insights did Jesus teach them?

6. What did they do as soon as they recognized Jesus?

READ LUKE 24:36–44

7. What emotions did the disciples express during their encounter with the risen Christ?

8. How did Jesus prove he had a body?

READ LUKE 24: 45–47

9. Where would this evangelistic effort begin and end?

The Ascension

READ LUKE 24:48–53

1. What did Jesus tell his disciples to do?

The Resurrection and Ascension: A Time for Rejoicing

2. After his ascension where did they go?

3. What did they do there?

The Significance of the Resurrection

READ MATT 28:18; EPH 1:19–23; PHIL 2:8–11

1. What authority does Jesus have now?

2. How did Jesus earn the right to rule?

READ HEB 1:3

3. Where is Jesus now?

Reflection: Are you rejoicing because you serve a risen Savior? Take time to thank him now.

Summary

Jesus appeared to his disciples over a period of forty days (Acts 1:3). After he ascended to heaven, Jesus sat down at God the Father's right hand. Jesus reigns from his throne in heaven over all creation, but especially his own, those he bought with his blood.

Just as the disciples rejoiced at Jesus' resurrection, some day believers will shout for joy at his second coming. Are you waiting for his return?

PART FOUR

The Church: Proclaiming the Promised Seed

Lesson 31

The Day of Pentecost: The Work of the Holy Spirit

For years I hid Christmas presents under my bed. When the children discovered my hiding place, they tried to get a sneak preview. The disciples could not do this. After Jesus' ascension, they had to wait ten days before receiving the gift of the Holy Spirit.

Question: How do you keep presents a surprise for your family?

The Work of the Holy Spirit before Pentecost

READ LUKE 1:13–15, 41, 67

1. Who did God fill with the Holy Spirit?

READ JOHN 4:4–10

2. What did Jesus offer the woman at the well?

READ JOHN 7:37–39

3. Who is the living water?

God's Unfolding Story of Salvation

READ JOHN 4:11–20

4. What kind of water was the woman looking for? Why?

5. Who would receive eternal life?

6. How did Jesus turn the conversation back to spiritual realities?

READ JOHN 4:21–24

7. What kind of worship pleases God?

READ JOHN 4:25–30

8. What truth did Jesus ask the woman to believe?

9. Who gave the woman the ability to believe this truth?

READ JOHN 4:39–42

10. When did the woman receive the gift of living water?

11. What did the Holy Spirit accomplish in that village?

The Day of Pentecost: The Work of the Holy Spirit

The Day of Pentecost

There are fifty days inclusive from the resurrection to Pentecost.[1] Jesus' followers saw him over a period of forty days (Acts 1:3). After his ascension they waited ten more days until Pentecost.

READ LUKE 24:52, 53; ACTS 1:12–14

1. Describe the behavior of the believers immediately after Jesus' ascension.

READ ACTS 1:4, 5

2. What did Jesus say would happen to the believers in a few days?

READ ACTS 2:1–4

3. What happened to the believers on the day of Pentecost?

READ ACTS 2:5–13

4. What visitors were in Jerusalem for the Passover?

5. What did the believers do after they had received the Holy Spirit?

6. How did the visitors react?

---

1. Fausset, *Fausset's Bible Dictionary*, 557.

God's Unfolding Story of Salvation

7. How did the baptism of the Holy Spirit change the believers' attitude toward others?

READ ACTS 2:14, 15, 36–41

8. How did Peter's sermon affect his listeners?

9. What did Peter tell them to do?

10. How many people did God save that day?

The Work of the Holy Spirit after Pentecost

READ JOHN 16:7

1. Why must Jesus leave his disciples?

READ JOHN 16:8–15

2. Who does the Holy Spirit always promote and exalt?

READ ROM 3:9–18, 21–24

3. Why does God judge everyone to be guilty of sin?

4. What does the Holy Spirit teach us about righteousness?

The Day of Pentecost: The Work of the Holy Spirit

READ ACTS 2:41; ACTS 9:31

5. What important work did the Holy Spirit begin at Pentecost?

READ ACTS 11:15–18 (PETER IS AT THE HOUSE OF CORNELIUS, THE ROMAN CENTURION); ACTS 19:1–5

6. What was the result of the baptism of the Holy Spirit?

Reflection: Has the Holy Spirit filled you with zeal to share the good news of salvation through Jesus alone?

Summary

Before Pentecost believers needed the indwelling of the Holy Spirit in order to believe in God and worship him. For example, the woman at the well received the living water that Jesus offered her. That was why she quickly ran into town and told everyone about Jesus. However the Holy Spirit did not come with power like a strong wind or impassable river until Pentecost. Few people believed before Pentecost. Afterward thousands trusted Jesus for salvation. This resulted in the formation of a visible spiritual community—the church, consisting of people from all over the world.

God calls the events of Pentecost, the baptism of the Holy Spirit. Like those first believers, whenever we trust in Jesus for salvation, we become part of the church. This is a one-time event in the life of every believer. Since Pentecost, the Holy Spirit has been joining believers from all over the world into one body in Christ. He did this to empower us to carry out the mission of spreading the Gospel to the whole world. Think of the impact of God working all over the earth through believers compared to Jesus living and preaching in a small-localized area.

LESSON 32

The Early Church: No Discrimination Allowed

AFTER PENTECOST THE YOUNG church met daily in the temple courts and listened to the apostles preach. Every day more Jews repented of their sins and accepted Jesus as their Lord and Savior. Many foreign converts remained in Jerusalem instead of going home, until persecution erupted.

Question: Why does it often take trouble before we do what God wants?

The First Persecution, AD 35[1]

READ ACTS 6:8–15

1. Who opposed Stephen?

2. What did false witnesses testify?

READ ACTS 7:51–54[2]

3. Why were members of the Sanhedrin so angry?

---

1. Maas, "A Chronology of Bible Events and World Events," 1940.
2. This is at the end of Stephen's speech to the Sanhedrin, the Jewish high council.

The Early Church: No Discrimination Allowed

READ ACTS 7:55—8:1

4. Who approved of Stephen's stoning?

5. What happened after Stephen died?

The Conversion of Saul, AD 35[3]

READ ACTS 9:1, 2

1. Why did Saul, also called Paul, go to Damascus?

READ ACTS 9:3–9

2. What happened to Saul just outside of Damascus?

READ ACTS 9:10–16

3. What was God's plan for Saul's life?

READ ACTS 9:17–22

4. How did Saul demonstrate God had changed his heart?

---

3. Maas, "A Chronology of Bible Events and World Events," 1940.

Peter and Cornelius

READ ACTS 10:1–8

1. Why did an angel appear to Cornelius?

2. What did the angel tell him to do?

READ ACTS 10:9–23

3. What was Peter's vision?

4. What did it mean?

READ ACTS 10:24–29

5. What was the Jewish attitude toward Gentiles?

READ ACTS 10:30–48

6. What important lesson did Peter learn?

Reflection: Do we only want to associate with people like us? God does not play favorites.

Summary

Saul is an example of God's sovereignty in salvation. He was on his way to Damascus to arrest Christians. Instead Jesus confronted Saul and prevented him from carrying out his wicked plans. By God's grace, Saul repented of his sin and accepted Jesus as his Lord and Savior. Thus Saul became a believer.

God also taught Peter an important lesson when he saved Cornelius. Gentiles could now become part of God's family in the same way as Jews by believing that Jesus died on the cross for them.

Lesson 33

Growth through Missions: Resolving Conflict

God relocates people from one place to another in order to grow his kingdom. My three children were not happy when we moved to a new city. But the Holy Spirit used the preacher at our new church to melt their hard hearts. They accepted Jesus as their Lord and Savior.

Question: Explain if a move has helped someone in your family spiritually.

The First Missionaries

Paul's first missionary journey, AD 46–48[1]

READ ACTS 11:19–21

1. To whom did the believers first preach?

2. What happened differently in Antioch?

READ ACTS 11:22–26

3. How did Barnabas encourage the believers at Antioch?

---

1. Maas, "A Chronology of Bible Events and World Events," 1940.

Growth through Missions: Resolving Conflict

READ ACTS 13:1–5

4. Who were the first missionaries whom the church officially sent?

5. To whom did they first preach?

READ ACTS 13:42–48

6. Why were the unbelieving Jews jealous?

7. How did Paul and Barnabas respond to their abusive talk?

8. How did the Gentiles react?

READ ACTS 14:26–28

9. What did Paul and Barnabas report to the church at Antioch?

The First Christian Council, AD 50[2]

READ ACTS 15:1–6

1. What trouble did some Jewish believers cause in the church at Antioch?[3]

---

2. Ibid., 1940.
3. These men were called Judaizers.

God's Unfolding Story of Salvation

2. How did the church decide to deal with this problem?

READ ACTS 15:7–11

3. How are Jews and Gentiles saved?

READ ACTS 15:12–21

4. Who convinced James that Gentiles did not need to be circumcised?

5. What happened to change his attitude?

6. How did James resolve this conflict over circumcision?

Reflection: How easily do you try to understand another's point of view in order to resolve conflicts?

Summary

Those first Jewish believers must have thought God was making a u-turn. They were God's special people. Now the Lord included Gentiles as his. What's more, Gentiles did not have to follow all the rules of Judaism.

Do you sometimes have difficulty accepting how the New Testament interprets the Old Testament? When God explains the Old Testament in the New Testament, we must listen. It is not optional.

Lesson 34

The Hope of Israel: A Believer's Hope

AFTER HIS THIRD MISSIONARY journey some Jews falsely accused Paul and had him arrested. Two years later, he appealed to Caesar for justice. Festus, the procurator of Judea, was unwilling to send Paul as a prisoner to Rome without reason. Therefore he asked King Agrippa for help.

Question: To whom do you go for advice? Why?

Paul's Arrest

Paul imprisoned in Caesarea, AD 57–59[1]
READ ACTS 21:17–19, 27–36

1. Why did the Roman commander arrest Paul?

READ ACTS 21:39—22:1; ACTS 22:19–29

2. Why did the commander need to be careful how he treated Paul?

---

1. Maas, "A Chronology of Bible Events and World Events," 1941.

READ ACTS 22:30; ACTS 23:6–11

3. Describe the beliefs of the Pharisees and Sadducees.

4. How did the Pharisees and Sadducees react to Paul's words?

5. What did God tell Paul afterward?

Conflicting Hopes

READ ACTS 26:1–8; DAN 12:2

1. Why did Paul emphasize he was a Pharisee?

2. What is the hope of Israel?

READ ACTS 26:12–23

3. What message of salvation did Paul preach?

4. What did the prophets and Moses foretell?

READ ACTS 26:24–32

5. How did Agrippa and Festus react to Paul's message?

The Hope of Israel: A Believer's Hope

6. Why did they send Paul to Rome?

READ GEN 49:10; 2 SAM 7:22–24; PS 2:7–9; PS 37:28, 29

7. How did most Jews interpret the fulfillment of these promises?

8. What kind of Messiah did they expect?

READ ACTS 2:29–33; JOHN 18:36; ROM 10:11–13; 1 COR 15:50–54

9. What kind of Messiah is Jesus?

10. Explain the conflict between the two hopes for Israel.

Reflection: What is your hope? Are you looking forward to eternal life with God or to earthly desires?

Summary

Philip Mauro explains this conflict best:

> Had he been preaching what the Jews themselves believed to be, and what their rabbis had given them as, the true interpretation of the prophecies (namely, that God's promise to Israel was a kingdom of earthly character which should have dominion over all the world) they would have heard him with intense satisfaction. But what Paul and all the apostles preached was, that what God had promised afore by His prophets in the Holy Scriptures was a

kingdom over which Jesus Christ of the seed of David should reign *in resurrection*, a kingdom which flesh and blood *cannot inherit*, a kingdom which does *not* clash with the duly constituted governments of this world, and one into which Gentiles are called *upon terms of perfect equality* with Jews . . .

Thus the teaching of Christ and His apostles in respect to the vitally important subject of the Kingdom of God, the hope of Israel, came into violent collision with that of the leaders of Israel; and because of this *He* was crucified and *they* were persecuted.[2]

---

2. Mauro, *The Hope of Israel: What Is It?*, 11, 12.

Lesson 35

Early Letters from Paul: Only One Gospel

TODAY IT IS POPULAR to believe in multiple ways to heaven. Since all world religions have merit, everyone will eventually end up together in the afterlife. But Jesus taught he was the only way to heaven. That is why Paul preached salvation through Jesus alone.

Question: How do you respond to people who think it does not matter what they believe?

To the Galatians

Date written: AD 49, from Antioch[1]

READ GAL 1:8; GAL 6:14

1. What was most important to Paul?

2. What did he think about anyone who disagreed with him?

---

1. Maas, "A Chronology of Bible Events and World Events," 2112.

READ GAL 4:21–31

3. Explain the relationship between the two women and the two covenants.

4. Which covenant is in effect today?

5. What are the implications of getting rid of the slave woman when considering the two covenants?

To the Thessalonians

1 Thessalonians written about AD 51, from Corinth[2]

READ 1 THESS 4:16—5:3

1. What will happen to believers and nonbelievers at Jesus' second coming?

READ 1 THESS 5:4–24

2. Summarize how believers should prepare for Jesus' return.

---

2. Ibid., 2169.

To the Corinthians

1 Corinthians
Written about AD 55, from Ephesus[3]

READ 1 COR 15:22–26

1. What will happen to believers at Jesus' return?

2. What will Jesus destroy at his second coming?

3. When will Jesus hand his kingdom over to God?

4. What is the last enemy to be destroyed? When?

READ 1 COR 15:50–54

5. What kind of bodies will believers have?

6. Explain why no one can die after his return.

---

3. Ibid., 2059.

God's Unfolding Story of Salvation

2 Corinthians

Written about AD 55–57, from Macedonia[4]

READ 2 COR 5:6–10

1. How will Jesus judge believers?

READ 2 COR 6:1, 2

2. Explain why no one can be saved after Jesus' return.

Reflection: Do you feel any urgency about sharing the good news of salvation to others? Why?

Summary

Paul encountered two problems in the early years of the church. First, Judaizers preached a false gospel by insisting on the circumcision of Gentile believers. To them, the cross of Christ was not sufficient to save a sinner. Their underlying problem was an unwillingness to give up the old covenant. Thus Gentiles could only approach God through Judaism. In the eyes of the Judaizers, all the terms and promises of the old covenant remained in force. Instead God, through Paul, clearly taught that the new covenant had replaced the old.

Paul's second problem concerned Jesus' second coming. When Jesus did not come back right away, believers became confused. They needed teaching on how to live and what to expect when he did return.

---

4. Ibid., 2091.

Lesson 36

Later Letters from Paul: Salvation through Jesus Alone

PAUL LONGED TO PREACH the gospel to the citizens of Rome in person. When he was in Corinth, he did the next best thing. He wrote them a letter.

Question: For whom are you praying? Why?

To the Romans

Date written: about AD 57, from Corinth[1]

READ ROM 3:23; ROM 6:23

1. How have we fallen short of God's glory?

2. What is the result of sin?

3. What does God offer the sinner?

---

1. Maas, "A Chronology of Bible Events and World Events," 2023.

God's Unfolding Story of Salvation

> READ ROM 5:6–8

4. How did God show he loved us?

5. Why did Jesus die?

> READ ROM 9:14–18

6. Who determines who will be saved?

> READ ROM 3:21–26

7. How does Jesus' death demonstrate God's justice and mercy?

8. Whose righteousness does God see when he looks at a believer?

9. How do we obtain this righteousness?

> READ ROM 5:1

10. Why does a believer have peace with God?

> READ ROM 12:1

11. How should we respond to God's wonderful salvation?

Later Letters from Paul: Salvation through Jesus Alone

To the Ephesians

Date written: about AD 60, from Rome[2]

READ EPH 1:3–10

1. What spiritual blessings belong to believers? Why?

READ EPH 2:1–10

2. Can a dead person come back to life on his or her own?

3. How does God show his great love for believers?

4. How does God demonstrate his sovereignty in salvation?

5. Why does God save sinners?

READ EPH 2:11–22

6. How are Jews and Gentiles reconciled to God?

7. What are the consequences and benefits of the union of Jews and Gentiles in Christ?

---

2. Ibid., 2128.

To the Philippians

Date written: about AD 61, from Rome[3]

READ PHIL 2:12, 13

1. Who enables us to keep on living for God every day? Why?

READ PHIL 3:1–11

2. Why does Paul consider his background as worthless as rubbish?

Reflection: God has a plan and a purpose for your life. Are you willing to obey him?

Summary

In his letters Paul answered many questions concerning salvation. What does it mean to be saved? Why do we need it? How do we receive it? Who can be saved? What happens after we accept God's gift of salvation? Therefore it is wise to study these letters carefully and ask the Holy Spirit to open our spiritual eyes so that we may understand God's marvelous gift of salvation.

---

3. Ibid., 2143.

LESSON 37

Letters from Other Authors: A Living Faith and Hope

BROUGHT UP UNDER THE law, the first Jewish believers struggled to understand the relationship between faith and works. Many Christians today have the same problem.

Question: Assume you grew up believing in the necessity of obedience to the law in order to please God. How difficult would it be to understand the relationship between faith and works?

From James

Date written: probably AD 49, before the first Christian council.[1]
Written by James, half-brother of Jesus and the first bishop of the church in Jerusalem.

READ JAS 1:22

1. How should we respond to God's word?

READ JAS 2:8–11; JAS 3:2

2. What does it mean to break one of God's laws?

---

1. Maas, "A Chronology of Bible Events and World Events," 2243.

3. Who has kept the law perfectly?

4. Explain why the law can never save a person.

READ JAS 2:17–22, 26

5. What is the proper relationship between faith and works?

6. Compare faith and works with the body and spirit.

From Peter

1 Peter

Written about AD 62–64, possibly from Rome.[2]

READ 1 PET 1:3–5

1. What is a believer's hope?

READ 1 PET 2:24; 1 PET 3:18

2. What did Jesus' death accomplish?

---

2. Ibid., 2254.

Letters from Other Authors: A Living Faith and Hope

2 Peter

Written about AD 67, three years after 1 Peter was written, possibly from Rome.[3]

READ 2 PET 3:8–10

1. What will happen at the end of the world?

2. Why has God delayed the end of the world so far?

READ ACTS 1:6–8

3. What did the apostles ask Jesus after his resurrection?

4. What was Jesus' answer?

READ 2 PET 3:13

5. What did Peter look forward to forty years later?

From the Writer to the Hebrews

Date written: probably before the destruction of the temple in Jerusalem in AD 70.[4] Writer unknown.

---

3. Ibid., 2266.
4. Ibid., 2217.

God's Unfolding Story of Salvation

READ HEB 4:1, 2, 7–11

1. What opportunity do nonbelievers have today?

2. What Sabbath rest do believers look forward to?

READ HEB 8:1, 2

3. Who is our high priest?

4. Where is he now?

READ HEB 9:11–14

5. Whose blood did Jesus present to God?

READ HEB 9:24–28

6. What did Jesus' sacrifice accomplish?

READ HEB 10:11–18

7. Compare the priests of the Old Testament with Jesus, our high priest.

8. How do you know if God accepted Jesus' sacrifice?

9. Compare the old and new covenants.

READ HEB 10:19–29

10. What is the hope of a believer?

11. What will happen to those who reject God's truth?

READ HEB 12:22, 23

12. Who belongs to the spiritual community of Zion?

Reflection: "And let us consider how we may spur one another on toward love and good deeds" (Heb 10:24).

Summary

For James, faith without works is dead. Our works do not save us, but we show we are saved by our works.

For Peter, faith is living and active. Moreover he waited expectantly for Jesus to usher in the new heaven and new earth. This is significant considering the fact that the disciples were more interested in a political kingdom at first.

The writer to the Hebrews yearned for Jewish believers to appreciate how superior the new covenant was over the old. Under the old covenant animal sacrifices could never take away sin. They only foreshadowed the perfect sacrifice of Jesus. After Jesus' death and resurrection, sacrificing animals would no longer be necessary, for the sinless Lamb of God shed his blood to pay the penalty for sinners. Moreover God has united all believers, past, present, and future, into the everlasting spiritual kingdom of Zion, the church.

Lesson 38

Revelation: Jesus, the Sovereign Lord

Probably about AD 95, by John from Patmos.[1]

Persecution under Domitian,
emperor of the Roman Empire: AD 90–95.[2]

SINCE PENTECOST, THE HOLY Spirit has been busy spreading the good news of salvation through the shed blood of Jesus. Although saved, believers often need reminding about Jesus' sovereignty and protective care over his own. This is the purpose of Revelation.

Question: When have you recognized Jesus' guidance or providence in your life?

READ REV 1:1–8, 17, 18

1. Who is the subject of this book? List some of his attributes.

2. What is the job of believers?

---

1. Maas, "A Chronology of Bible Events and World Events," 2295.
2. Ibid., 2295.

3. What will happen at Jesus' return?

READ REV 1:12, 13, 16, 20

4. Who and what does Jesus have authority over?

READ REV 5:1–10

5. Why did Jesus have the right to open the scroll?

READ REV 6:1, 2; REV 19:11–16; PS 45:4–7

6. Who is the rider on the white horse?

7. With what weapon does he rule the nations?

READ REV 6:3–8; ZECH 1:8–10

8. Describe the job of these three horses in Revelation.

9. Who sent them?

READ REV 11:15–19

10. What events will occur when the seventh trumpet sounds?

God's Unfolding Story of Salvation

READ REV 12:1–9

11. Who was born?

12. Who was defeated in this battle?

READ REV 12:10–17[3]

13. What gives Jesus the right to be sovereign?

14. How may believers defeat the schemes of Satan?

15. Who is in control during times of persecution?

16. Why can Satan never destroy the church?

READ REV 6:15, 16; REV 14:14–20; REV 16:15–21; REV 19:11–21

17. What will happen to nonbelievers at the end of the world?

READ REV 19:6–10

18. What will happen at the wedding supper of the Lamb?

---

3. When the Jews revolted from Rome in AD 66, the Christians in Jerusalem fled to Pella. In AD 70, Titus destroyed Jerusalem, but the Christians were safe.

Revelation: Jesus, the Sovereign Lord

19. Explain the meaning of "the testimony of Jesus is the spirit of prophecy."

READ REV 20:11–15

20. Who will God judge at the great white throne? How will he judge them?

21. Why do believers not need to fear this judgment?

READ REV 21:1–7

22. Who will inherit the new heaven and new earth?

READ REV 21:22–27

23. Why will there be no need for a temple there?

READ REV 22:1–5

24. Describe paradise restored.

READ REV 22:12–16

25. What does Jesus want the churches to know?

Reflection: "The Spirit and the bride say, 'Come!' And let the one who hears say, 'Come!' Let the one who is thirsty come; and let the one who wishes take the free gift of the water of life" (Rev 22:17). It is not too late. Have you accepted God's marvelous gift of salvation?

Summary

This book was a comfort to the persecuted Christians back in John's day. It provides the same encouragement for us. Through John's visions, we catch a glimpse of the spiritual world where Jesus reigns supreme over all creation. He earned this right because of his death and resurrection. But notice how he especially cares for his own.

We also see how God controls the life span of people through sickness, war, and famine. In fact, nothing happens that he does not allow. Even evil cannot thwart God's will. At the end of time God will inaugurate a paradise superior to the Garden of Eden. Sin will never have a chance to enter there, and God will dwell with his redeemed people in peace, forever.

Final Thoughts

Congratulations, you have finished this journey through the Bible. May you be humbled knowing how God the Father sent his only Son whom he loved to die for sinners. May you rejoice because Jesus became the perfect substitute to take our punishment. May knowing God always keeps his promises strengthen your faith.

I also hope you have a better understanding of the big picture in the Bible. It is a Christ-centered storyline. It is God's plan for our salvation made manifest in the birth, death, resurrection and exaltation of his son, Jesus Christ. Before creation God determined to carry out his plan of salvation. This was his only focus, for his glory and our benefit. The result will be a redeemed people living forever with him. Knowing these truths, do you have an overwhelming desire to reach out to others with the good news of salvation through Jesus alone before he returns? If so, then this book has fulfilled its purpose.

Timeline

Redemptive History in the Old Testament

Adam and Eve
Cain and Abel
Enoch
Noah and the flood
1951–1776 BC Abraham
Melchizedek, contemporary of Abraham
1851–1671 BC Isaac
1791–1644 BC Jacob (Israel)
1446 BC Escape from Egypt; formation of Israel as a nation
1406 BC Entering the Promised Land
1375–1050 BC Ruth lived during the time of the Judges
1010–970 BC David's reign
970–930 BC Solomon's reign
930 BC Kingdom divided into two—
      the northern kingdom of Israel
      and the southern kingdom of Judah
874–853 BC Elijah: Confronting Baal's prophets in Israel
      during the reign of Ahab
835–796 BC Joel (from Judah): Preaching to Judah
785–760 BC Jonah (from Israel): Preaching to Nineveh
760–750 BC Amos (from Judah): Preaching to Israel
753–715 BC Hosea (from Israel): Preaching to Israel
742–687 BC Micah (from Judah): Preaching to both

Timeline

740–681 BC Isaiah: Preaching to Judah

722 BC Fall of Samaria, capital of Israel, by Assyria

640–621 BC Zephaniah: Preaching to Judah

627–586 BC Jeremiah: Preaching to Judah

612–589 BC Habakkuk: Preaching to Judah

605–536 BC Daniel: Written in Babylonia

593–571 BC Ezekiel: Written in Babylonia

586 BC Fall of Jerusalem, capital of Judah, by Babylonia

538 BC Edict of Cyrus: God's people may return home and rebuild the temple

520 BC Haggai: Exhortation to build new temple

520–480 BC Zechariah: Exhortation to build new temple

516 BC Temple rebuilt

458 BC Ezra taught the people the law of God

445 BC Nehemiah rebuilt the walls of Jerusalem

430 BC Malachi: Announcing arrival of the promised seed

Redemptive History in the New Testament

6/5 BC Jesus' birth

AD 26 Ministry of John the Baptist

AD 26/27–30 Ministry of Jesus

AD 35 Martyrdom of Stephen, First persecution

AD 35 Conversion of Saul (Paul)

AD 46–48 Paul: First missionary journey

AD 49 James, written by Jesus' half-brother, James

AD 49 Galatians, written by Paul

AD 50 First Christian council at Jerusalem

AD 51 1 Thessalonians, written by Paul

AD 55 1 Corinthians, written by Paul

AD 55–57 2 Corinthians, written by Paul

AD 57 Romans, written by Paul

AD 57–59 Paul imprisoned in Caesarea

Timeline

AD 60 Ephesians, written by Paul
AD 61 Philippians, written by Paul
AD 62–64 1 Peter, written by Peter
AD 67 2 Peter, written by Peter
Before AD 70 Hebrews, author unknown
AD 70 Destruction of Jerusalem
AD 95 Revelation, written by John

Bibliography

Fausset, A. R. *Fausset's Bible Dictionary*. Grand Rapids: Zondervan, 1949.

Kendall, Heather A. *A Tale of Two Kingdoms*. Belleville, ON: Guardian, 2006.

Maas, David. "A Chronology of Bible Events and World Events." In *Life Application Study Bible*. Wheaton, IL: Tyndale, 1991.

Mauro, Philip. *The Hope of Israel: What Is It?* Swengel, PA: Reiner, n.d.

Piper, John. *Desiring God*. Colorado Springs: Multnomah, 2003.

Price, Ira M., Leslie E. Fuller, and Chester J. Attig. "Synchronous History of the Nations." In *The New Standard Alphabetical Indexed Bible*. Chicago: Hertel, 1963.

Robertson, A. T. *A Harmony of the Gospels for Students of the Life of Christ*. New York: Harper & Row, 1950.

Robinson, Theodore H. "History of the Hebrew and Jewish People." In The Abingdon Bible Commentary. Eds. Frederick Carl Eiselen, Edwin Lewis, and David G. Downey. New York: Abingdon-Cokesbury, 1929, 60–72.

Wallace, D. H. "Messiah." In Evangelical Dictionary of Theology. Ed. Walter A. Elwell. Grand Rapids: Baker, 1984, 710, 711.

www.ingramcontent.com/pod-product-compliance
Lightning Source LLC
Chambersburg PA
CBHW071447150426
43191CB00008B/1261